THE ART OF DARKNESS

THE ART OF DARKNESS
Staging the Philip Pullman Trilogy

Robert Butler

Oberon Books

The Author

Robert Butler is a freelance journalist. From 1995-2000 he was drama critic of the *Independent on Sunday*. He is the author of two books in the series 'The National Theatre at Work', *Humble Beginnings* and *Just About Anything Goes*, and the Methuen commentary on Michael Frayn's *Copenhagen*.

Copyright © The National Theatre 2003

Published in 2003 by the National Theatre
in association with Oberon Books Ltd
www.nationaltheatre.org.uk/publications

Oberon Books (incorporating Absolute Classics)
521 Caledonian Road, London N7 9RH
Tel: 020 7607 Fax: 020 7607 3629
oberon.books@btinternet.com
www.oberonbooks.com

The National Theatre and Robert Butler are hereby identified as authors of this book in accordance with section 77 of the Copyright, Designs and Patents Act 1988. The authors have asserted their moral rights.

ISBN: 1 84002 414 3

Quotations from Philip Pullman's *Northern Lights*, *The Subtle Knife* and *The Amber Spyglass* Copyright © Philip Pullman
Quotations from the play script of *His Dark Materials* Copyright © Nicholas Wright

Rehearsal and production photographs by Ivan Kyncl *(IK)*
Workshop photographs by Charlotte MacMillan *(CM)*
Cover design by Michael Mayhew/Louise Forrester, photograph copyright © Jerry Uelsmann (courtesy Laurence Miller Gallery, New York)

Other books in the 'The National Theatre at Work' series are: Jonathan Croall's *Hamlet Observed, Inside the Molly House,* and *Peter Hall's Bacchai*, and Robert Butler's *Humble Beginnings* and *Just About Anything Goes*. Di Trevis' *Remembrance of Things Proust* also explores the process of putting on a play at the National.

Typeset in Helvetica Neue
Printed in Great Britain by G&B Printers, Hanworth, Middlesex

Acknowledgements and Thanks

DURING THE FIVE YEARS I spent as the drama critic for the *Independent on Sunday* I usually had 1000 words a week in which to review three or four plays. Imagine trying to describe *His Dark Materials* in a few hundred words (it will be done). But after my stint as a critic I was keen to find another way of writing about theatre. I am very grateful to Lyn Haill, the editor of the 'National Theatre at Work' series, for commissioning me to write about a production at considerably longer than 1000 words, and thereby giving me the chance to approach a production from many different angles.

Many thanks to Nicholas Hytner for his encouragement and stylish *write-what-you-like* attitude; to Philip Pullman and Nicholas Wright for permission to quote from *His Dark Materials*, the novels and the plays; and to the entire company of *His Dark Materials* for their warm tolerance of an observer with a reporter's notebook in the rehearsal room. I hope this account reflects the range and depth of talent involved.

Inside and outside the rehearsal room, everyone used first names. It seemed closer to the atmosphere of rehearsals to do the same in the book. I apologise to readers who feel uneasy about this informality. I have not named stage managers as there were two stage management teams, four in each, and it would have required its own chapter to do justice to their roles.

On a personal note, I have been going to the National – under various guises – since soon after it opened in 1976. For 40 years my parents have lived in a flat which is a ten minute walk from the theatre, so as a teenager, in the Seventies, it was my luck that the National was my local rep. In the Mid-Eighties, I worked there as an assistant to the director Michael Rudman; during the Nineties, I reviewed many productions at the National; and in the 2000s, I have written three accounts of productions for the 'National Theatre at Work' series. Like countless thousands of others, I have been a long-term beneficiary of the campaign for a National Theatre that was begun a hundred years ago by three people, William Archer, Harley Granville Barker and George Bernard Shaw, all of whom wrote at length about theatre.

A number of people have read or discussed sections of the book. I am indebted to Marie-Christine Willis, Tim de Lisle, Kellie Gutman and Anthony Holden. My thanks also to Rosie Beattie for finding me a place to work (the dressing room next to Mrs Coulter no less), to John Langley (for the book's title), to Lucinda Morrison and Mary Parker in the press office, to James Hogan and Ian Higham at Oberon, to Nick Marston and Joe Phillips at Curtis Brown. My love and thanks to my brother William, for his comments from Los Angeles, and to my wife Sarah, daughter Lucy and son Sam, for most things else.

15 September – 15 December 2003
National Theatre, SE1

Contents

No-Name	What can you do for me?
Lyra	We could tell you where we've been. You might be interested.
No-Name	You mean, you'll tell me a story?
Lyra	Yeah.
No-Name	Tell me a story I like, and I might let you through.

His Dark Materials, p.207

The pleasure for me was in not knowing how the story was going to end.
Philip Pullman, on his first efforts as a nine-year-old storyteller.

All page numbers refer to the play text of *His Dark Materials* by Nicholas Wright (Nick Hern Books)
Warning: the following account gives away major plot details.

Chapter One

"...each entered the forest where it was darkest and where there was no path."
La Queste del Saint Graal

ANNA AND SAM had agreed to meet first at Waterloo Station. You can overdo nerves, of course. They weren't about to rob a bank, or run into a burning building to save a screaming baby, or parachute behind enemy lines. It wasn't as bad as that.

From Waterloo the two of them crossed Stamford Street and walked towards the River Thames. It was warm for mid-September, Sam wore a T-shirt, Anna had orange flip-flops: not your average clothes for the first day of a new job, but this was not your average new job. Anna and Sam stepped into the shade provided by a row of concrete buttresses, and turned into a side-entrance.

Sam collected a swipe card from the desk and followed Anna through the security door. Anna had worked here many times before,

Above: Anna Maxwell Martin *(IK)*

but Sam hadn't, so when Anna turned left, turned right and went through a door, Sam simply followed. It was important that Anna and Sam got on very well as they were going to be spending nearly every day of the next six months together. The people who had hired Sam knew how close he was to Anna. The two of them had met five years ago on their first day as students.

At the end of the corridor, Anna turned right again, went through another door and turned left. The place was a rabbit warren. Each corridor glowed with same pale light. "I'll never remember this", said Sam. "You will," said Anna, taking a left at a payphone and heading through another door. She sighed, "This is the bit I dread." She took another right and went through another door.

Anna knew there were people all over the country who had their own idea of what it was she was about to do. There was stuff on the internet already. There were millions of people out there who knew what anbaric was, or naptha, or who had heard about smoke-leaf, cloud pine and chocolatl, gyrocopters, armoured bears and daemons. They knew all about Lyra too. Anna was determined not to let these people down. She would be as faithful as she could. But right now, it was the people inside the building, not the ones outside, who were making her feel apprehensive.

Anna and Sam went through two more doors and entered a room the size of a warehouse. It was called Rehearsal Room One. They pushed through a crowd of fifty people that hung around the doorway. In the middle of the room stood Nick, a wiry figure in jeans and a grey shirt – the smile on his face was anbaric.

Nearly the last person to enter the room was a tall, dark, handsome man – middle-aged, now – wearing a dark jacket, dark shirt and dark trousers. His face had been on posters all round the world. He had the wary look of someone who has faced hordes of photographers. The very last person to enter the room was a man whom quite a few people there had never seen before. He had a pink shirt and green socks, a broad face and glasses, and his thinning grey hair was swept back to reveal a domed forehead. His smile had more of a naptha glow. In his way, he was as famous as the tall, dark, handsome man.

Nick, the wiry one with the anbaric smile, asked people to sit in the circle of chairs that had been arranged in the centre. Nick didn't exactly sit down himself, he crouched on his seat, feet under his knees, as if he were about to take a big leap forward – which he was.

More than anyone else in the room, he knew the risk that was about to be taken. He wasn't going to spell it out to the actors around him but he had admitted to a journalist months ago that this could easily not work. He could be wrong about the whole thing.

The people who had gathered in that rehearsal room were going to be doing something that seemed very simple. They would be telling a story. If they could make it exciting, if they could make people care

Above: Philip Pullman *(IK)*

about what happened to the characters, it would work. Easy enough, in theory.

This story would follow two twelve-year-olds as they travelled between universes. They would meet terrifying creatures called harpies, spectres and cliffghasts. They would journey to the Land of the Dead and they would take part in a battle between the angels in heaven. They would witness the death of God and – to some people's horror – these two twelve-year-olds would fall in love and spend the night together.

The author, Philip Pullman, had told this story across three novels called *Northern Lights, The Subtle Knife* and *The Amber Spyglass*. The title for the whole trilogy, *His Dark Materials* was going to be the title for two plays, *His Dark Materials – Part One* and *Part Two*.

The books had sold nearly three million copies, been translated into 36 languages and had a devoted body of fans. Some readers had even said the books had changed their lives. As a director and producer, this was the sort of challenge Nick liked. He had told another journalist that he was aiming these plays at a sullen fifteen-year-old who had read the books, been dragged along to the theatre, and was sitting there, arms folded, waiting to disagree with everything.

If Nick had to boil the whole story down to a single sentence he would say it was about a young girl looking for love. She doesn't know it, but she's lonely. She wants to be loved and she wants to love. That single thread would be the audience's way into the whole story. Nick was going to make sure that at every twist and turn of the story this girl called Lyra was put in the greatest possible peril. Lyra was going to be played by Anna.

Everyone in the rehearsal room that morning knew that they would have to take great care not to lose the whatever-it-was these books had. Otherwise they could turn out to be alchemists in reverse: start off with gold, experiment with it for ten weeks, and end up with base

metal. One by one, round the circle, they introduced themselves. Nick went first.

"I'm Nick Hytner," he said, "the director." The man with the pink shirt and green socks was sitting on his left. He said, "I'm Philip Pullman, I wrote the books." Next to him sat the man in the dark jacket, dark shirt and dark trousers. "I'm Tim Dalton," he said, "playing Lord Asriel." (Fans of *Living Daylights* and *Licence To Kill* had been hoping he was going to say, "The name's Bond. James Bond.") An elegant woman, currently appearing in a TV series, was teasing out strands of her coiffured hair. Her shirt, her trousers and her shoes were creamy white. Her skin was porcelain. Her watch, bracelet and hair were golden. "I'm Patricia Hodge," she said, "playing Mrs Coulter."

A third of the way round the circle, Anna introduced herself, "I'm Anna Maxwell Martin – playing Lyra." Another third of the way round, Sam said, "I'm Sam Barnett – playing Pantalaimon." Near him sat a young man, with tousled black hair, a two-day stubble and electric blue trainers. If Lyra was the hero of *Northern Lights*, Will was the hero of *The Subtle Knife.* Together they were the heroes of *The Amber*

Above: Dominic Cooper and Anna Maxwell Martin, Niamh Cusack in the background *(IK)*

Spyglass. "I'm Dominic Cooper," he said, "playing Will." Dominic knew Anna well, and he knew Sam well too. Five years before, they had all been at drama school together.

● ● ●

AS SOON AS NICK was appointed to run the National Theatre – this was in 2000 – he had decided that he wanted to do a play for a young audience. So many shows for younger audiences seemed like dinosaurs from another age. *Alice in Wonderland* was written in 1865, the year Abraham Lincoln was assassinated. *The Jungle Book* was written in 1894, *The Wizard of Oz* in 1900 and *Peter Pan* in 1904. *The Wind in the Willows* – which Nick himself had directed in this theatre – was written in 1908. It wasn't until twenty years after *The Wind in the Willows* that women under 30 were allowed to vote in Britain. These plays were from another age entirely, they probably appealed more to the grandparents or even great-grandparents of today's young audiences.

Nick wanted to do a play that spoke as directly to a young audience as a movie at the local multiplex. He didn't know what the play he wanted to do would be about, he only knew what it had to be like. It was a colleague of his, Jack Bradley, the National Theatre's Literary Manager, who recommended he read *His Dark Materials.* Anyone who has read the books might have thought that this was Jack's idea of a joke.

Nick would not have to get very far into *His Dark Materials* to see that it was almost impossible to stage. The text of any play is a mixture of speeches and stage directions and most plays contain fairly simple stage directions, along the lines of 'he enters the room' or 'she picks up the phone' or 'he lights a cigarette.' People who prefer plays to novels sometimes argue that novels are plays with too many stage directions.

Top: Dewi Wynne (ASM) and Helen Murton *(IK)*

Bottom: Patricia Hodge and Inika Leigh Wright *(IK)*

His Dark Materials has lines that could never work on stage the way they do in print. "The bird's head exploded in a mist of red and white". That's a short moment that looks tough to stage, but here's an even shorter one, "The cat stepped forward, and vanished". When Nick reached the big descriptive passages he was surely going to chuck the books aside and look for something else. There was no chance, for instance, that he could stage Philip Pullman's panoramic description of the arrival of the witches:

> "All through the day the witches came, like flakes of black snow on the wings of a storm, filling the skies with the darting flutter of their silk."

Even if he did dream up a way of doing that, he would be defeated by the later moment, when Lord Asriel shoots down a zeppelin, and Asriel and Mrs Coulter watch it fall on an area where a bomb has exploded:

> "they watched as the blazing zeppelin fell slowly, slowly down on top of the whole scene, bomb, cable, soldiers and all, and everything began to tumble in a welter of smoke and flames down the mountainside, gathering speed and incinerating the resinous trees as it went, until it plunged into the white waters of the cataract..."

The entire budget for the production would have to be spent on a single paragraph. Nevertheless, Nick took Jack's advice and he was halfway through the first volume, *Northern Lights*, when he said, "Yes, this feels like it", and halfway through the second volume, *The Subtle Knife,* when he said to Jack, "Let's get the stage rights". Taking risks is essential in the theatre, and the decision he had just taken was high risk. "It's one of those things that if you hesitate," Nick said, "You don't do. It felt crazy, it felt unstageable, but I felt we had to try."

● ● ●

THREE YEARS AFTER he took that decision, Nick was sitting in Rehearsal Room One looking at the cast of *His Dark Materials.* Another theatre director has said that Nick's oval face and arched eyebrows make him look like a mime artist. Over the next ten weeks it was going to be hard to think of someone who talked so freely as having the face of a mime. This morning, though, he was going to let others do the talking. "I'd like us to take a deep breath," he said, "and go straight into the new draft of Act One."

Chairs scraped closer together, throats cleared, pages rustled, as everyone skimmed past two pages that listed the characters and settled on page three. The stage directions said the scene was the Botanic Garden in Oxford. It was night, there was a tree with spreading branches and a clock was striking twelve. The first person to speak a line of the new play was Anna.

"Will?" she said.

In the rehearsal room the sun poured down from some high windows and fell like a spotlight on Philip Pullman. He put on an old sunhat to keep out the glare. As he listened, his teeth squeezed the tip of his thumb. He had been writing books for thirty years and, out of all the characters he had written, the one Anna was playing was his favourite.

The second person to speak was Dominic.

"Lyra?"

Dominic playing Will, told Anna playing Lyra, that he missed her, and he missed Pantalaimon too. In fact, he missed Pantalaimon as much as he missed Lyra, "Because he *is* you."

Then Sam, who was playing Pantalaimon, told Anna/Lyra that she had to say something to Dominic/Will.

Hang on! This was the first page of the first play and already things were getting weird. On this page alone two big ideas needed explaining. If this had been on video, it would have been possible to rewind it and watch it again, hitting the pause button frame by frame.

– of the three people in this conversation two of them appeared not to be able to see the third. They were in the same scene and they weren't in the same scene.

– Will says, "Because he *is* you." If Pantalaimon is Lyra, then Sam and Anna have been hired to play the same character.

The play opens when Lyra and Will are in their twenties. Turn to the next page and Lyra is twelve. (When Will enters the plot eighty pages later, he is also twelve.) So a story about two twelve-year-olds, Lyra and Will, was going to be played by two actors, Anna and Dominic, both in their twenties.

On the second page, Lyra is fighting with brickburners' kids and Gyptian kids; on the fifth page an Oxford professor gives a lecture on the force connecting a human being to his daemon; on the sixth, a priest arrives in Oxford from Geneva and attacks the academics for thinking thoughts not approved by the Church. Wherever this Oxford was, it was not the one that could be found by leaving the National Theatre and driving up the A40.

The cast read the first act of the first play. During the coffee break Philip Pullman said goodbye and left. Nick explained that Pullman had gone to meet the Archbishop of Canterbury. Pullman had spent seven years writing *His Dark Materials* in a shed at the end of his garden, and now he was barely able to get to rehearsals (which he wanted to do) because he was so busy meeting people, appearing on TV and radio and giving interviews to publicise his next book.

It took the rest of the morning to finish the second act. Nick liked the way the actors playing children hadn't done any child-acting. "At 2.30," Nick said, "There are going to be lots of other folk here." The cast filed out of Rehearsal Room One into the maze of corridors and staircases that make up the National Theatre.

● ● ●

WHEN WE FIRST meet Lyra in *His Dark Materials*, she lives in Jordan College, Oxford, where she had been adopted by the Master and Fellows, and where she roams freely around the college grounds. The twelve-year-old Lyra likes to clamber over the college roofs, spit plum stones on passing scholars and hoot like an owl.

Imagine, for a moment, if things had been a little different and Lyra had gone to live in another large institution, but this time, one in London. Imagine if Lyra had been adopted by the chairman and board of the National Theatre.

She might not have minded. It is a big place and there would be dozens of new worlds for her to explore within this one building. It is possible to get so far into the National Theatre that you have no idea whether you would need a coat or umbrella when you got outside. For someone with a taste for fantasy, and for going through doors marked 'Danger – Authorised Personnel Only', it might be irresistible.

If Lyra had followed the cast out of rehearsals that first morning she would have gone up some stairs and along some corridors to the canteen, which is open all day. Lyra never has to cook or wash up at Jordan College. She wouldn't have to here either. In the bar next door, which is called the Green Room, and is the only place inside the building where smoking is allowed, Lyra could listen to actors telling stories about touring plays, or appearing in TV series, or filming in exotic locations. Every actor knows a famous actor and has a story to tell. In the Green Room there were people who could tell stories as tall as Lyra's.

Along the corridors, things could get deliciously weird. Lyra might pass two of the actors from the Harry Potter movies: the woman who played Madame Hooch and the man who played Gilderoy Lockhart were both in the building. Or she might pass a New York gangster, a French courtesan or a Victorian gentleman on their way back to their dressing rooms. She might hear a blazing row going on inside a room and not know whether this was a scene from a play. She might pass a

Top: John Carlisle *(IK)*

Above: Jamie Harding *(IK)*

man wearing a dark suit and a dog collar and have no idea whether he was an actor playing a vicar or the theatre chaplain. There was a constant turnover of people, with new actors regularly arriving to do new shows, and there were nearly always some children around.

Lyra wouldn't have wanted to hang out on the fourth and fifth floors, with their uniform offices, names and titles outside the doors, and computer screens, swivel chairs and shelves of folders inside. No, it was another part of the building that promised adventure. Lyra would head off down a wide indoor passage (painted with yellow stripes) called 'the Drum Road'. In the workshops along this road, sets were built and painted, props made and special effects devised by teams of engineers, carpenters, carvers, sculptors, painters and electricians.

In the securely locked armoury department, Lyra would find daggers, rifles and machine guns. Upstairs, in the costume department, there were piles of fabrics and racks of clothes. In the wig department, she could choose between the blow-dried hairstyle of a society hostess or the dreadlocks of a Rastafarian. If she had gone to the very top of one of the staircases, beyond the fifth floor landing, past a sign saying 'access to the roof is absolutely prohibited', she could have stepped onto the gravel surface of the roof, and seen the London Eye, Battersea Power Station, Crystal Palace, Blackheath. The view went on and on.

The quietest place in the whole building was underground in the sound studios. None of the walls here was directly attached to the wall of another studio, so no sound could penetrate. Inside was absolute silence. Once Lyra had switched on the computer and clicked on the files, she could play around with train crashes and nuclear explosions and wolves howling in a forest at night. If she wanted, she could play with half a dozen recordings of a barn owl (every bird was here), slow up the recording, move it down an octave, and come up with something that would really keep people awake. It was possible to stay all night in a sound studio. Time dissolved in this underground world and Lyra would only know it was 8pm because that was when the air conditioning went off. The one thing that drove the sound designers out of these studios (when they were up against a deadline) was the heat. The later it got, the hotter it was.

There was no doubt that the darkest place in the building was inside something called the Drum. There were three theatres within this one building, the biggest of which was the Olivier. Underneath the Olivier stage sat a huge machine called the drum revolve. To reach it you had to go through doors marked 'Danger!' and 'Authorised Personnel Only'. When the lights were off, there was no darkness to compare with it. If Lyra had stood at the bottom of the Drum at that moment she would have had the dizzying experience of losing all sense of space. It was crushingly dark in there.

The Drum was like a dustbin that went down under the stage for sixty feet. Lyra could have stood on a platform at the bottom of this bin and machinery would have carried her all the way up to the top. If this had been in the middle of a performance, she would have found herself taken up to the stage level and standing in front of a thousand people.

If Lyra ever tired of exploring the workshops, she could always watch a show from backstage. As she stood in the blue half-light of the wings, she would be able to see the look on actors' faces, as they made last-minute checks in the mirror. Before they went on, some actors would stand for ages, locked in concentration, while others hurried towards their entrance, as if late for a train. Sometimes Lyra might have seen actors rush offstage after a crowd scene and run towards people called dressers, who were waiting with clothes. Actors playing passengers on a cruise ship (for instance) would run off, put on trousers, coat, scarf and hat on top of the clothes they were already wearing, turn round and go straight back onstage as newspaper reporters. It had taken only a few seconds to change from one character to another. From the wings, Lyra could see the light reflecting off the stage and onto the rows and rows of the audience. Their faces shone with anticipation. It made everyone look younger.

To maintain her sense of privilege, Lyra could slip through one of the many security doors to the Front of House. Here she could mingle with the audience as they bought drinks and read programmes. As she eavesdropped, she would have the pleasure of knowing that those around her had only the faintest idea about the backstage world from which she had emerged.

Here was a building large and rich and various enough for a twelve-year-old. Wherever Lyra went, she would find people who were among the best in the world at what they did. These people were working in all sorts of areas, doing highly specific jobs, often jobs that Lyra wouldn't have imagined existed. Someone was carving polystyrene into trees. Someone was laying a series of air-jets along the floor of the stage and covering each jet with sand, so that when activated, it looked like a round of machine-gun bullets hitting the beach. Someone was recording the sound of an audience chatting inside a theatre, so that when the real audience actually arrived for a play, there was a gentle hubbub of chat going on that made the place feel warm. The thrill of the building was that it was full of people working hard at something grown-ups don't usually take seriously. They were in the business of telling stories. The place was a factory of make-believe.

● ● ●

AT 2.30 THE NUMBER of people in Rehearsal Room One had doubled. They had come from all over the building to the 'meet and greet', when everyone involved has to say who they are and what they do, and the director talks about the plans for the show and unveils the model of the set. On this occasion, there was a mass of a hundred people in the room, so that when the time came for everyone to say who they were, Nick had to divide the group up into half a dozen

blocks, otherwise no-one would have known when it was their turn to introduce themselves.

He said he was delighted to see so many here. This was the biggest group he had ever seen in a rehearsal room and he felt that was absolutely right. He had never directed two plays at the same time before, and he wanted as many people as possible to be involved, as these plays were going to draw on every available resource within the building. Between now and the press night they were going to have to mount something like a military campaign.

He stood next to a black box that was the model of the set. Next to the black box was a white box, packed with miniature trees, benches, desks, tables, chairs, crates, a tower and a balloon. There would be more than a hundred scenes in the stage version of *His Dark Materials*. One of the basic aims, he said, was that it would be a show that never stopped. Every change between one scene and another had to happen at great speed. "If you have a hundred scene changes and

Above: Richard Youman, Andrew Westfield, Stephen Greif, Daniel Tuite and Jason Thorpe *(IK)*

each takes thirty seconds," he said, "Well, you can work it out for yourself..."

When it came to the real thing, stage machinery would be moving the benches, trees and tables round with effortless speed. With the model of the set, all the little fiddly pieces had to be moved by hand. "It's going to take as long for me to show this to you," he said, "as it would for you to watch the show." He picked out some highlights, but for the hundred people watching this little lecture, even for Anna, who was sitting in the front row, it was confusing. The enthusiast in Nick wanted to explain how more and more of the scenes were going to work, "I think I'm losing you," he said, as the storyteller in him won through, and he moved on to the next subject.

He went on to explain to the actors that he wanted a style of acting he called 'high definition'. He wanted the characters to be large and distinctive, to stand out against a dramatic landscape. He mentioned two films from the 1940s, both directed by David Lean, that had high definition acting – *Great Expectations* and *Oliver Twist*. He warned that rehearsals were going to be brisk. There would not be a limitless amount of time to ask questions.

Some very sophisticated special effects were planned, with video footage, slides and fibre optics, but other things would be simply done – the daemons, for instance. Ever since Nick had announced he was going to direct *His Dark Materials* people had been asking him one question: how are you going to do the daemons? The biggest challenge in staging the books appears in the opening sentence: "Lyra and her daemon moved through the darkening Hall…"

In the parallel universe in which the first volume begins, every person has a visible daemon, an animal that embodies the soul, subconscious or inner feelings of the character. That opening sentence would have made most directors look elsewhere. With the mention of daemons, it was time for Nick to finish his introduction and hand over to Jeff.

Jeff Curry is an American with a tan and white teeth, who works on the West Coast. His brother Michael runs the Michael Curry Studios in Portland, Oregon, where the daemons were made. (It was Michael Curry who made the puppets for the stage musical *The Lion King*.) Everyone followed Jeff over to a row of trestle tables and formed an orderly queue. "It's like a buffet," someone said. The black cloth on the tables was divided into squares by tape and in each square stood a daemon. They didn't look exactly like animals.

The surface of each creature's face and body was translucent. A fabric had been stretched and moulded over wires to give shape to the ridges, hollows and planes around the eye sockets, cheeks and jaw lines. The wire outlines made the creatures light and airy. The fabric itself was painted in muted browns, greens, oranges and yellows – crisp autumn colours. These were ghostly creatures with friendly faces. They didn't look like Disney characters.

As James Bond, Timothy Dalton had become accustomed to productions going to huge expense to achieve special effects to keep people at the edge of their seats. This was another approach. "It struck me right at the beginning of rehearsals," he said, "that here you are, looking at a bit of bent wire and curtain material, and you invest it with personality, you feel for it, because it has a story."

The name of each creature was written in capitals. It was easy enough to spot 'FROG' and 'SPIDER', but an actor would need to be pretty good on animals to identify 'LEMMING', 'LEMUR' and 'MUSKRAT'. The one with a wide face and a pointy nose, like a stern interviewer, was 'OWL'. The one with dry bony features, like a balding civil servant, was 'VULTURE'. The one with sharp black ears, mischievous green eyes and a red mouth, who looked like he might hang around nightclubs, was 'WILDCAT'.

Jeff explained that the idea was that all the daemons had characteristics in common. They hadn't wanted the puppets to represent live animals, or to be fully fleshed-out, they wanted them to

Opposite: Timothy Dalton *(IK)*

look as if they came from a spirit world. He picked up one daemon after another and demonstrated (to 'oohs' and 'aahs' from the actors) how the puppet worked. The movements were always 'subtle', everything else about them was 'kinda fun'.

Jeff picked up one daemon the size of a terrier. This was the one, he said, that had determined the look of the show. It had an earnest open face as if it was someone's best mate. Either that, or it was staring into the headlights of an oncoming car. This was 'PINE MARTEN'.

Sam was particularly interested in this one because pine marten was one of the shapes taken by Pantalaimon. What he had liked about the pine marten in the books was that he was affectionate, wrapped himself around Lyra's neck and comforted and warmed her. Sam hadn't looked the pine marten up in any nature videos or made a trip to London Zoo, so he couldn't judge if what he was looking at that afternoon resembled a pine marten or not. But he liked its face, which looked bright and cheeky and young, the way Sam imagined Lyra in the first book.

Above: Patrick Godfrey *(IK)*

Lyra's daemon doesn't settle into one shape until the end of the story, so there would be other creatures that Sam would use: the wildcat, the hare, a little bird, the moth and the butterfly; but the pine marten, the one who had determined the look of all the others, would be the main one he would be acting with over the next six months.

Jeff switched on the little bulb inside the pine marten's head so that the face lit up. Sam could see there was almost nothing inside the pine marten except for a handle where he would put his index and second fingers to control the head. He would have to hold the battery pack in his palm and his thumb would rest on top, where it could control the light switch. Pantalaimon was one of the major characters in the story, so Sam was studying this puppet, wondering what he would be able to do with it. He could see he would be able to move the head from side to side, but it didn't really move up and down; it didn't nod, just shook.

Matt Wilde, the assistant director, told Sam that, at a show in Plymouth, a woman in her fifties had come up to him and asked, How are you doing Pantalaimon? When Sam heard this, he thought, "God, it is... it is a responsibility to get it right. To really give some magic to this daemon. People really treat him as a proper character." He certainly wasn't burdened with any preconceived ideas. "I've never done anything like this before. And I haven't seen anything like it done."

All the way through that afternoon, as Nick and Jeff gave their talks, the costume designer, Jon Morrell, had been sticking drawings of the costumes up on the wall. There were dozens of them. Next to the drawings, he would sometimes pin up a photograph from a magazine or history book that had inspired the drawing. As the young Lyra, Anna would start out wearing a pinafore, knitted jersey and plimsolls and change into a party dress, an eskimo coat, hospital garments and so on.

However much the costumes changed, it would be what goes on inside Lyra that would make the story a real adventure. In *Northern*

Lights, we learn that she is proud, fidgety, healthy, thoughtless, stubborn, a barbarian, a half-wildcat and a coarse and greedy little savage. At the start of the trilogy, Lyra is on the cusp of adolescence, so many of the things that we learn about her at the start of *Northern Lights* have changed by the end of *The Amber Spyglass.* Anna would have to be true to a Lyra who changes on her journey from innocence to experience, and to the moments when she undergoes those changes.

If Lyra were the same person at the end of the second play as she is at the beginning of the first, her character would be of no interest to Anna or to the audience. These days, people are used to travelling, and often the impact their journeys have is fairly insignificant. Lyra's adventures are the opposite kind. She won't be coming back with a slightly better tan. Her travels will change her on the inside as much as the outside.

Pullman knows Lyra's age group very well. For twelve years he taught English to children between the ages of nine and thirteen. It would be Anna's job to be like one of those children in his classes. Anna wasn't a child, but she could try to catch the energy a twelve-year-old has, to think in the way a twelve-year-old thinks, and to become someone immediate and instinctive who says what she feels.

● ● ●

TWO DAYS LATER several members of the cast were sitting in a semi-circle in the rehearsal room looking at some pages of the script. Anna, Sam and a couple of other actors had studied a photograph of the set model, read a scene, and now they were discussing it. The scene in question was the opening of the book ("Lyra and her daemon moved through the darkening Hall...") when Lyra and Pantalaimon sneak into the Retiring Room, hear someone coming and hide in a cupboard. From their hiding place, they witness the Master of the College attempt to poison Lord Asriel. The scene that opens the book has to wait ten pages in the play to allow for some scene-setting about Lyra's life in Oxford, Lyra meeting with her new friend Roger, and the arrival of Lord Asriel.

After they read the scene, there was a pause and Nick said, "That suggests lots of things." He spoke in the soft thoughtful way that directors often use at this point in rehearsals. (That would change.) He said Anna and Sam would need to speak in the same Oxford accent and use the same speech rhythms. "We're looking for the idea that they are one."

Nick wanted to work out what Pantalaimon was thinking and what Lyra was thinking. He was always looking for the actors always to play strong clear emotions. He said he wanted Sam to be more "front-foot", and the pair of them to be "quite spunky with each other".

Above: Samuel Barnett, Anna Maxwell Martin and Dominic Cooper *(IK)*

They had hit a central question: what was the relationship between Lyra and her daemon Pantalaimon? Anna said, "My feeling is that it changes depending on who Lyra is talking to."

Nick said, "I've a feeling, Sam, that Pan's very often the one who says 'bad idea – don't do that.'"

"It's strange," said Sam, "Pan gets scared independently of Lyra and she comforts him."

Anna agreed that Lyra and Pantalaimon had separate thought processes. "It's almost a brother-brother or sister-sister thing, where the older one doesn't want to show fear in front of the younger one."

Sam suggested a rigorously clear-cut distinction. "One is acting as the head and one as the heart." But Anna thought it was even more complicated than that. "Sometimes he plants thoughts ahead of her,'" she said. "The thoughts are there somewhere but she hasn't got to them yet." The whole relationship between a daemon and a person was going to be hard to unravel. Anna said, "People don't always like what their daemons become. The daemon can show you things that you may not like about yourself." Nick recalled the story in the first book about the man whose daemon settles as a dolphin, so, reluctantly, the man is compelled to spend his life on the sea.

Sam mentioned yet another way that the relationship between Lyra and Pantalaimon worked. If Lyra was with someone she didn't like, or who frightened her, she might deliberately try and hide her feelings. But Pantalaimon's behaviour would be 'the vehicle' for showing the audience how scared Lyra was. He would be the one revealing her inner feelings. Pantalaimon was almost... but, no. Nick said, "Philip won't go so far as to say the daemon is the soul."

Like many aspects of the book, a daemon was rich in meaning, which was another way of saying, it couldn't be readily defined: a daemon could be the head or the heart, an older or younger brother or sister, the inner feelings someone isn't showing, or an instinctive intelligence, a sixth sense, that understands things before a person does. A daemon could almost be that person's soul, but not quite. Whatever a daemon was, Nick said, "You can't pin it down."

On Day Three, this was how things stood. Daemons had never before been presented on stage, no-one knew for certain how they would be done and no-one could even agree on what a daemon was. Sam could do little more than shake his daemon's head from side to side. He couldn't even move it up or down. In the simplest possible language available to a puppet (moving the head) he would be able to say no, but not yes.

When it came to what they were going to have to do, the cast of *His Dark Materials* were working in the dark. There was no-one they could copy and little they could refer to, because no-one had done this before. They were like knights in an old French romance for whom

Above: Jason Thorpe and Andrew Westfield *(IK)*

taking risks and entering the unknown were a source of pride. In the medieval tale, *The Quest for the Holy Grail*, each knight had to enter the forest "where it was darkest and where there was no path". It was a good motto for a theatre company. Staging *His Dark Materials* over the next nine and a half weeks was going to be that sort of adventure.

● ● ●

Chapter Two

"If I knew how to omit, I should ask no other knowledge."
Robert Louis Stevenson

A FEW DAYS BEFORE I met Philip Pullman, a friend e-mailed saying "Pullman everywhere". He was right; there had been a stream of articles about Pullman, and now he was on television too. The BBC was running a competition, *The Big Read,* for the most 100 most popular books of all time, and *His Dark Materials* was up there in the top five. Pullman was competing against Jane Austen, Tolkien, J. K. Rowling and... I forget who... Emily Brontë, probably.

A television profile on *The South Bank Show* had left the impression that his years as a school teacher had been formative. Pullman has the air of a man who has worked on his answers (has probably answered the question before; someone was always putting their hand up in class and asking that one), and who wouldn't be stopping and starting, breaking off in mid-sentence and starting another thought entirely. In this respect, his manner was exactly opposite to the director, Nick Hytner's, for whom every thought was a temporary sketch, to be almost immediately erased, sometimes rubbed out before it had been uttered, and replaced by another one.

When the stage version of *His Dark Materials* opened in December, it would be largely a combination of the work these two storytellers working in completely different fields – one whose job was filling a blank page, the other's to fill a vast stage. It was striking that their manner of talking was so dissimilar. They were physically dissimilar too: one large, relaxed and thoughtful; the other, compact, angular and with quickfire impatience. One had worked alone in his shed for seven years years; the other ran an organisation employing seven or eight hundred people.

I didn't know, as I drove to Oxford to meet him, that The Man Who Was Everywhere, was actually on the radio giving an interview. As it was, I had the cassette playing and was listening to Pullman anyway, as he narrated the audiotape of *His Dark Materials*, with a cast of actors playing the characters. The audiotape of the three books lasts 35 hours. The two plays that the National Theatre were staging would run for six. The maths was stark. Whatever else they would be doing, the National would have to drop 29 hours from the story. Five out of six sentences would have to go.

Needless to say, with those odds, the section of the story I was listening to was not going to end up in either of the plays. As the narrator, Pullman was introducing a moment when the powerful African commander, King Ogunwe, explains to the increasingly desperate Mrs Coulter that the Authority was not the creator of the world, someone else created it, and only later was there a battle in heaven between the angels. "At some point the Authority took charge," the deep-voiced Ogunwe tells Mrs Coulter, "and since then, angels have rebelled, and human beings have struggled against him too. This is the last rebellion."

The tape was building towards the battle between those angels who were on the side of the Authority (or God) and those who were against. King Ogunwe didn't make it into the plays, but the battle in heaven definitely did. The books were a rewrite of *Paradise Lost*, Milton's epic poem which describes the battle among the angels, when God defeated Lucifer, and cast him into hell. In *His Dark Materials* the tables are turned and the other side wins. Pullman also rewrites the *Book of Genesis* and this time the Adam and Eve characters achieve something wonderful by making love. These were provocative changes. The *Catholic Herald* said that his books were "worthy of the bonfire" and the *Mail on Sunday* described Pullman as "the most dangerous writer in Britain".

Opposite: Owl daemon *(CM)*

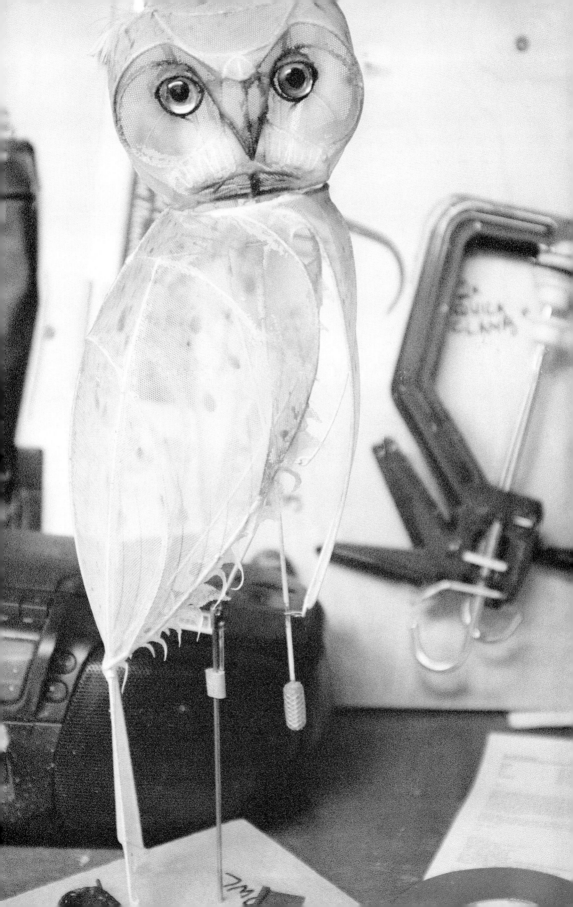

On the tape Pullman sounds more reassuring than dangerous. What is distinctive about his voice is his tone of gentle insistence. Stephen Greif, who plays the President in the two stage plays, also played Metatron on the audiotape. Stephen has recorded many books, so I asked him to describe Pullman's voice. He said "It's a soft voice, a cloudy voice, a professorial voice, an internal voice. It's a writer's voice. They are spoken thoughts."

For the last few years Pullman has been the most famous writer to work in a shed since Roald Dahl. Nearly every article about him has carried a description of the inside of his shed, which contains several hundred books, a guitar, a saxophone, a computer, decorated with brightly-coloured artificial flowers and a six-foot-long stuffed rat, which was the main prop in a play Pullman wrote called *Sherlock Holmes and the Limehouse Horror.*

Pullman went to Oxford as a student and came back, seven years after graduating, to teach. He has lived here for thirty years. Since writing *His Dark Materials,* he no longer works in a shed. He has moved to a farmhouse a few miles outside Oxford. The move to the countryside has brought new responsibilities. When I arrived at his house, his wife, Jude, showed me into the study next to the kitchen, because her husband was dealing with a mouse that had been caught in a trap and wasn't dead. Two pugs, Hogie and Nellie, nuzzled round my ankles. At first meeting, the most dangerous writer in Britain appeared to be mainly a threat to field mice.

In some ways, the room was a traditional writer's study – hundreds of books, comfortable chairs, papers everywhere, and a smart Applemac on the desk. But it also seemed to be a carpentry workshop. There were lathes, power drills and blocks of wood. On the floor lay a magazine about 'routing' (that's all about carving grooves in wood). In the centre of the room lay sections of a rocking horse, which Pullman was making for his grandson. He insisted, with characteristic precision, that he was a joiner, not a carpenter. Nearby, some oak

Opposite: Ben Whishaw/Kaisa *(IK)*

legs, that will support the oak table he was also making, leant against a wall.

A glance at the shelves, and the books on the floor, revealed many of the influences that had fed into *His Dark Materials*: Milton's *Paradise Lost*, poetry by Blake and Keats and the letters of George Bernard Shaw. Rival translations of Homer's *The Odyssey* sat in a pile, next to several editions of a comic called 'Love and Rockets'. The gold lettering on a heavy old red-bound edition of *Paradise Lost* (twice the size of a phone directory) advertised the illustrations by Gustave Doré.

On a sidetable was a long article in an American publication about the discovery of ancient Christian texts in Egypt, at Nag Hammadi, in 1945. It was not hard to imagine that these writings resonated strongly with the religious content of *His Dark Materials*. One of the works discovered was *The Gospel of Thomas,* which offers a fascinating variation on traditional Christianity. It includes the words "The Kingdom of the Father is spread upon the earth and men do not see it." In *The Gospel of Thomas,* Jesus also says, "Split the stick, you will find me there." That sense of wonder, of having a visionary relationship with the world as it is, and not with some other world, some afterlife that might be revealed to us after death – this is a central theme in *His Dark Materials*. On the final page of the trilogy Pullman writes that "where we are is always the most important place". This is where, in the final lines of the books and the plays, Lyra has to build the Republic of Heaven.

On the far wall of Pullman's study was a reproduction of 'Portico with Lantern', a painting by Canaletto of a deserted town, which inspired the setting for the streets of Cittàgazze where Lyra first meets Will. On the wall next to the computer, was a photograph of the National's Lyra and Will, Anna and Dominic – the first publicity shot for the production, taken right at the beginning of rehearsals.

A few days before driving to Oxford, I had gone into a bookshop near the National Theatre, and seen *Northern Lights, The Subtle Knife* and *The Amber Spyglass* sitting on a shelf among the 'Ps', between Marcel Proust's *A La Recherche du Temps Perdu* and Mario Puzo's *The Godfather*. On that shelf, the three books had beautiful paintings on the covers suggesting dark and secretive themes. Over on the other side of the same bookshop, *Northern Lights, The Subtle Knife* and *The Amber Spyglass* sat between Terry Pratchett and J K Rowling. On that shelf, the three books had sparkly, dazzling covers suggesting adventure and wizardry.

With *His Dark Materials* Pullman had found a way of writing for people who want sombre moody paintings on their front covers as well as for people who want sparkle and dazzle. I wanted to ask how he had discovered the ability to write books that ended up in two parts of the same bookshop. Adults find the stories every bit as absorbing as children, but his adult readers aren't wanting to be children for an hour or two, nor are the children trying to be especially grown-up. What was the secret? It was clearly going to be important that the stage production achieved the same thing.

I had read on the internet that the film company that had made *The Lord of the Rings* had bought the film rights to *His Dark Materials* and commissioned Tom Stoppard, who won an Oscar for *Shakespeare in Love*, to write the screenplay. I had also read that when Pullman was a teacher he had written the school plays, and that he had first begun telling stories when he was a child in Australia, sharing a room with his younger brother. This was the place where we started.

"I was about nine and he was two years younger. When the light went out, I used to start telling a story. The pleasure for me was in not knowing how the story was going to end when I began it."

When you moved to Wales, and went to school there, did you do plays?
"The teacher who taught English, Miss Enid Jones, used to put on a play every year, at Christmas time. It was the most enjoyable thing of the whole year at school."

Was it the acting you enjoyed?

"I enjoyed showing off; I'm sure I was a very poor actor. In fact, when I came up to Oxford I didn't take part in any of that. I did other things instead, like painting and gambling, and playing folk music."

What did you do between leaving university and becoming a teacher?

"I worked in a library, I worked in shops, I worked in offices. I was a sort of bum, really, drifting around, writing all the time, but not really wanting a career. Finally, it was borne in upon me that my writing was not going to earn any money for a very long time."

When you started teaching, how did it come about that you wrote the school plays?

"I wanted to do a play because I'd had such fun with them when I was at school and they'd never had a school play in that school before. The thing about a school play is that there is none of this nonsense with 'oh you can't afford more than three actors.' Have as many as you can get on the stage! The other thing is you were entertaining the parents as well as the children. And you do want to entertain them. I didn't want to have them surreptitiously looking at their watches and sighing heavily and wondering if the pubs would still be open when they got out. I wanted them really involved, and really excited by the story.

"You could fake it by having a lot of silly slapstick for the children and clever wordplay for the adults that passes over the heads of the children, so you're talking to two separate audiences at once, but I've never enjoyed that. I don't like it in the work of others and I've never done it myself. It's patronising, it's divisive, and it betrays a fundamental lack of sincerity in what you're doing. I wanted to entertain everyone in the same way."

What were the plays about?

"I wrote something about a Victorian hero of penny-dreadfuls called Spring-Heeled Jack. The next year I did an Arabian Nights fairy tale that I'd made up called *The Magic Feather*. My imagination was seized by the idea of genies and minarets and beautiful princesses and magic, so I wrote a play to bring all that in. The third year we did a Gothic story called *Count Karlstein*, which I later made into a novel. I did that because I wanted to use an effect that the chap we'd hired our lights from had told me about. He'd just got it and was very excited about it, as was I when he told me about it. It was a soft flickering hellfire effect. So we hired this thing from him at enormous cost and I wrote the play to build up to this scene of flickering hellfire. It was terrific."

Did you ever think of doing a play set today?

"How dull! No. Ordinary clothes? No. I wanted costumes. I wanted colour and spectacle. My source for all this was the toy theatre. Those lovely little things that you can get from Pollocks. I've got the lot. I discovered them when I was grown-up and fell in love with them."

Were you aware of moments when you misjudged your two audiences?

"I got better at it as it was going on. It's to do with taking the story seriously. Laughing, yes, but not laughing at it, never scoffing at it. Always taking the story seriously."

Why do you believe theatre is so important for young people?

"Well, I'll go back a bit and start with this point. Never before have so many people, including children, spent so long sitting watching other people pretend to do things. On the telly, of course. So I'm conscious that children, especially these days, with the television set in the bedroom, and so on, have enormous experience of watching drama. But it's drama on a screen. It's drama that is distant from you because of that. You can turn it off, you can flick the channels, you can turn the sound off. You can ignore it, because it's sort of separate from you.

"Now the huge importance of live theatre is that you are in the same physical space as the actors. You can see the lights; the light that falls on them is reflected off them onto you – it's the same light. You're in the same physical space; you hear their voices and it's the real voice you hear. They go clumping over the stage, you hear it. All the physical stuff, this is what a lot of children are starved of. They're starved of a physical engagement with the world. So when children go into a real theatre and see real people doing dramatic things in front of them, there's an engagement with it that's almost visceral."

When the National Theatre asked to do His Dark Materials*, what did you think?*

"I was astonished. I was somewhere in Scotland, doing an almost never-ending book tour. My agent called and said that Nicholas Hytner was interested. I was absolutely thrilled, of course. Delighted. And simultaneously relieved that it wasn't me having to make it into a play. It was someone else."

Did you think they had an impossible task?

"No. I don't think anything is impossible in the theatre. A very difficult and big task, yes, because they had to rethink it in theatrical terms. It's much easier probably to make a novel into a film because both have the ability to move immediately, instantaneously, from a wide-angle shot to a close-up. Of course there ain't no close-ups in the theatre. It's got to be conceived differently from the start. The cinema can easily show a polar bear wearing armour, who can stand up and talk and manipulate machinery. And they can show witches flying through the air and balloons sailing across the Arctic skies, very very easily. To do those things in the theatre you need to reconceive it in theatrical terms. It has to become metaphorical not literal, in a way."

Do you enjoy having your stories retold by other people?

"I'm fundamentally a storyteller, not a literary person, if I can make that distinction. I'm more interested, fundamentally, in the events I'm talking about than in the fine prose in which I recount them. I'm all for fine prose. I try to make my own as euphonious and interesting as I can. But the 'making up' part is always closer to my heart than the 'writing down' part. If I wrote a story that had enough vigour and life in it to pass into a common currency and be recounted by people who had no idea that I was the author of it, nothing would give me more pleasure."

How does reading your stories in a book differ from following them on stage?

"When you are reading a book you are in control of the speed you read at, and indeed even the order in which you read it. You are in command. Another way in which you are in command is that you supply the pictures when reading, you have to, so you're contributing.

"When you're watching somebody acting it out, the visual stuff is done for you, you don't have to contribute that. And you are not in control of the time either. The play will start at eight o'clock whether or not you are in your seat, and you can't say, 'Stop! Stop! Slower! Slower! Do that bit again!' So you surrender a certain amount of control.

"But what you gain in exchange is the sense of a joint experience. You're experiencing it together with all these other people. When you're reading a book you're alone and there are great values in that. But when you're in a theatre, and something transforming occurs, enchantment settles over the whole audience. That's something which you can't get by yourself."

After the interview, Pullman gave me the map of Oxford that appears in his new book *Lyra's Oxford* and photocopied a map of the real

Oxford. It was a five minute drive to see the Oxford that had inspired Lyra's Oxford: in North Oxford, there were the claybeds where Lyra loved to fight, and the roundabout by the avenue of hornbeam trees, where Will cuts a window into another world. In the centre of Oxford, there was Exeter College, where Pullman had gone as an undergraduate, and which was loosely the model for Jordan College. Not far away was the Botanic Garden. It was a bench in the Botanic Garden that the adapter, Nicholas Wright, the third storyteller in this group, had chosen for the start and end of the plays.

●●●

A WEEK LATER I spoke to Nicholas Wright about how he had set about adapting the books for the stage. His most recent play, *Vincent in Brixton*, about the time the young Van Gogh lived in London, had won an award as Best Play of the Year. Wright was a familiar figure

Above: Robert Butler, Nicholas Wright and Philip Pullman *(IK)*

within the National, because he had been the theatre's literary manager and an associate director.

Over the last two years there had been three workshops for *His Dark Materials*, where groups of actors had read scenes from the plays, as well as one full reading two weeks before the first rehearsal. After each workshop Wright had gone away and written another draft.

Since rehearsals began, Wright had attended nearly every day. In the rehearsal room he could sometimes be heard murmuring to himself. He was trying out a new line. When he wasn't there, he was at home writing a new scene. There were constant rewrites. On one occasion actors were handed a whole new version of Part One only to find that another rewrite, done that day, also needed to be included.

It was the novelist Robert Louis Stevenson who said, "If I knew how to omit, I should ask no other knowledge." Wright had a tremendous amount to omit. Many of the characters from the novels do not appear in the plays. The most important one to have been cut is the Oxford scientist Mary Malone – along with the whole section about the land of the mulefas at the beginning of *The Amber Spyglass*. The idea of staging creatures that move around on wheels seemed one headache too many. Other characters to have been cut include the Authority's right-hand man, Metatron, the head of St Sophia's, Dame Hannah Relf, the pale and trembling zealot, Father Gomez, and the commander of the angels, Xaphania. Pullman and Wright discussed the effect of cutting Mary Malone as she has a central role in the story. In the plays this role is giving to another character.

Rehearsals have been full of discussions about the script to ensure that the several quests remain at the forefront of the audience's mind. It was a process that Timothy Dalton enjoyed. "I've always thought the only point of being an actor," he said, "is to tell stories." This was Dalton's first time at the National and his first stage appearance for 14 years. "Spending the last 20 years in movies, where people are always writing and rewriting as you go along, it's something I'm terribly used to."

Several weeks into rehearsal an article appeared on the front page of *The Times Educational Supplement* saying that the Association of Christian Teachers had denounced Philip Pullman's books and the National's production, "His blasphemy is shameless… Teachers should steer clear." The Bishop of Willesden was more broad-minded. "The books put questions about life, death and morality on the agenda. It's much better to be talking about religious questions than ignoring them." The article was stuck up on the noticeboard outside the canteen. Members of the cast gathered round and read it. Several of the actors said, "Brilliant." Nick Hytner had told another newspaper that the National Theatre was not a church and it wasn't the National Theatre's job to celebrate Christmas.

I spoke to Nicholas Wright in the restaurant at the National Theatre. I wanted to know why he thought *His Dark Materials* would make a piece of theatre (at first glance they were unlikely novels to adapt), what kind of plays he thought his adaptations might turn out to be, and whether they were anti-religious. He talked first about how he had come across the books.

"Nick Hytner asked me about three years ago if I'd read the books, and I said yes, I thought they were incredible page-turners and could make a play or a big theatre event. I didn't know at that stage the National had any plans to do them. Nick rang me months later to say that they now had the rights and would I like to do the adaptation. I said yes immediately. I said yes on the phone."

Did you know when you started what kind of play you would be writing?
"No, not at all. The draft we're doing is something like the fifth. Each draft has been a less literal following from the book. I must say every departure from the book has been wrested from us, almost unwillingly, but it's always been in order to make it more of a play

that I've had to depart from the stories as the books tell them. I started by following the books very literally, picking scenes out which I thought would tell the story. But then as the logic of the plays took over, they changed more and more with each draft."

What were your first steps?

"I knew we would have several workshops to explore the way the production would work. I have to say *not* to have done it through a series of workshops would have been completely certifiably insane. This is not a project you could do through producing a script and having a chat with the director from time to time. It's just far too complex. I got a friend to compile an index, so that every bit of information about every character, every setting, every scene in the books, was put together. At the same time I did a page-by-page synopsis of the book. Then I did more synopses. And more synopses. Then I did a rough draft which was a basis for the first workshop. That was a lot to do with the conceptual ideas of the production. How the sets would be done. What kind of conventions the daemons would be in. Things like that."

How early on did you decide on the flashbacks?

"In synopsis-stage, at the suggestion of the friend who was doing the index. It was always fundamental to Nick's vision of the show that Will and Lyra and the other children would not be played by children but by young actors. Of course telling the story in flashback has the effect of rationalising that. So that was pretty basic."

Several of your plays have been done in the West End and in America, what future could you see for His Dark Materials*?*

"Usually, when you write a play you hope it will get lots of productions or maybe transfer to the West End or go to America. Well, with this play, you can just forget all that. Because professionally, I would say, it's more or less completely tied to the National Theatre. There's no other theatre that could put on a production of this scale or has the stage that could take it. Except you could also do it with nothing at all. There's nothing to stop anybody doing it in the school hall. No problem at all. It's a great show for kids to produce. They can make their own daemons. They can do whatever they like."

What made you think the books might make a play?

"The whole aspect of Lyra's journey and her growing up, and the philosophical questions about death, responsibility, friendship, morality, God – all these things lend themselves enormously to a play for young people. I remember from my own childhood just how much those questions interested me. The last thing any of us wanted to lose from the show was that moral seriousness and questioning; that's what makes it not just the adventure of a little girl meeting lots of strange characters. It has to be a story that throws up the kind of serious questions that young people think about and really want to know about. The question everybody goes through, for example: if there's a God, why does he allow bad things to happen? Again that has to come up in the play. If God is a character in it, which he sort of is, you have to raise that question."

Are the books anti-religious?

"The books are unambiguously anti-clerical and so are the plays. But it's hard to think of books that celebrate the numinous and the inexplicable and the mysterious quite so vividly. I don't find them anti-religious books. I find the books, and I hope the plays are the same, extremely respectful of people's need to find symbols for the important things in life, growing up, and dying, and falling in love and all those things. There's no disregard for faith in the books at all. What there is, is a very restless sense that people's approximations to the spiritual life are inadequate. They become hardened and calcified and dreary and untruthful. Deformed. But who would disagree with that?"

At this point in the interview, someone approached Nicholas Wright to say hello. It was Sir Tom Stoppard. For a moment it looked as if the man who had written the movie version might be about to sit down with the man who had written the stage version and they could compare notes about which bits they had decided to omit. (The only person who had read both versions was Pullman himself.) Half a dozen questions sprang to mind. Would the movie version include the war in heaven and the death of the Authority? Since 99% of Americans say that they believe in God, it might be box office poison to make a film that depicts the death of God. The movie would have to use twelve-year-old actors: what would they do about filming the scene when the two twelve-year-olds lose their sexual innocence? Could he confirm the rumour that the first ten minutes of his film were devoted to a history of the alethiometer? And was it true that Nicole Kidman was going to play Mrs Coulter? So many questions! But Stoppard saw the tape-recorder sitting on the table, between the ashtray and the glasses of wine. "Oh no," he said, "interrupting an interview. How gauche!" and he moved along the bar.

● ● ●

Chapter Three

"The great consult began."
Milton, *Paradise Lost*

"THE THING I KEEP thinking I'll solve in rehearsal," said Nick, looking at a model of the set, "is Mrs Coulter's first appearance. What's she doing? Is she reading the paper?" He was at a meeting in Kilburn with the set designer, Giles Cadle, the costume designer, Jon Morrell, and – the only woman at the meeting – the lighting designer, Paule Constable.

From the outside, passers-by in Kilburn could see only some frosted windows between a dentist's and a kebab shop. Inside, Giles'

Above: Jon Morrell (costume designer) *(CM)*

studio looked like a cross between an architect's office, with drawing boards, plans and models, and the 'oversize' book section of the local library: hundreds of hefty art books lined the shelves. Some lay open on the tables, references marked with post-it notes. An architectural guide to Oxford was open at a page showing photos of Exeter College and the post-it note said "spikes" and "spires". A book about Antarctic explorers was open at a photograph of a ship stuck in the ice. The post-it note said, "ice up balloon rigging".

The creative team crowded round the model of the set as Giles moved the miniature pieces around the stage. They were weeks and weeks away from the first day of rehearsal and Nick and the designers were already sorting out entrances and exits. It was like directing a major movie, where (as screenwriter William Goldman once said) most of the work is done before the filming starts. By the first day of rehearsal, Nick had fixed a good deal of what the audience would be seeing on the first night.

The schedule was alarmingly tight, as Nick explained to the others. They would rehearse *Play One* for three weeks, then *Play Two* for three weeks, then *Play One* for a week and a half, then *Play Two* for a week and a half. Then they would go back to *Play One* for two or three days, then *Play Two* for two or three days. "We need to have *Play Two* absolutely cooking," said Nick, "Because we don't do it for two weeks and then we have three days before its first preview. Scary. Really scary."

By this stage of the summer, the adapter, Nicholas Wright, was free to rewrite the scenes over and over again (as he would do) but he could not change their order. That had to be fixed so that Giles could get the sets made. Designing the transitions between scenes – how the set for one came off the stage and the following went on – was as big a job as designing the scenes themselves.

The use of silhouettes would be central to Giles' overall design: the silhouettes would move around (on trucks), changing the shape and mood of the stage. For instance, there were half a dozen separate Oxford scenes. "Oxford just gets rearranged every time," said Giles. With a hundred scenes, it wasn't possible to bring on bulky sets. The scenes would alternate between exteriors and interiors. "You close in and you open up," said Giles, "You open up for the big landscape moments." The interiors would come up on the stage or room inside the drum revolve, which everyone had decided to refer to as the *droom* (drum + room). "The whole thing is to keep it going," said Gilles, "Never stopping."

Nick and the designers looked at the models for the bench and the tree in the Botanic Garden, where the grown-up Lyra and Will meet at midnight. "They plainly spend six hours together," Nick said, "because we spend six hours with them. They part at dawn." They looked at outdoors Oxford where the children fight and where Lord Asriel arrives. The model of the dank green College walls stood out against the circular backdrop, known as the cyclorama, or 'cyc'. Giles was avoiding the warm honey colours that people associate with Oxford architecture.

"The world she starts off in looks a bit like Aberdeen," explained Nick.

"A bit granite," said Paule.

"It should be quite a threatening world from the start," said Giles.

"It's there in the silhouettes," said Paule, "Shall we discuss the 'cyc', while it's here?"

"It's going to have to do a lot of work," said Giles.

"It's very big," said Paule.

(It would need a lot of lights.)

"And it moves," said Giles.

(They couldn't attach lights to it.)

"And there's no depth behind it," said Paule.

(It couldn't be lit from behind.)

Slides would be one answer. "You need to feel the sky can go wild and epic," said Nick, "I'm sure Oxford is a peaceful blue sky with fluffy white clouds. But when you're in *Play Two*, for instance, the clouded mountain world, then you can almost go sci-fi."

The skies would change from the chilly northern skies of Trollesund to the Mediterranean warmth of Cittàgazze.

"It's about temperature," said Giles.

"Not only literal," said Paule.

"But psychological," said Giles.

"Yes," said Paule.

After the Retiring Room, where the Master tries to poison Lord Asriel's drink, they reached the scene in the Master's study, where Lyra is summoned to be told that a wealthy widow has offered to take her to live in London. Lyra immediately objects, and Mrs Coulter enters, saying, "May I speak to her?" It was a downstage scene, the actors would be standing close to the audience.

"In the movie," Nick said, "she would just walk in from behind the shadows or through an open door."

"We couldn't use darkness," said Paule.

(It's almost impossible to make a downstage scene dark.)

"It's two people, don't forget," said Nick, "There's the Golden Monkey. Maybe the Golden Monkey could come on first."

"Is the Golden Monkey a person?" asked Paule.

"Yes," said Nick, "We may not need the Pan actor. Lyra might be able to take the puppet as she comes in."

Where would Mrs Coulter enter? What lighting would there be? What music? What would she wear? Mrs Coulter's entrance was only one of a hundred moments that they discussed. Jon, the costume designer, had brought his display folios and they went through the sketches and magazine photos. He didn't want the clothes to draw attention to whether the puppeteer was male or female. The twelve-year-old Lyra would start off looking like a Fifties schoolgirl. The

Church would be a combination of purple ecclesiastical robes and totalitarian uniform. The witches would be strong, spiky and primitive with sticks, feathers, leather and home-made skins. "There should be a beauty to them," Jon said, "striding through the forests and riding the storms." Lord Asriel would have old tweeds under a trenchcoat. He would be a bit Indiana Jones, a bit like a World War Two flying ace. And Mrs Coulter? "The glamour should never be pushed so far that it says this woman is false," Nick said, "She's like a favourite aunt. Every kid has that fantasy that an aunt will whisk them away from their boring humdrum lives and show them a good time."

On the first day of rehearsals, Jon pinned his drawing of Mrs Coulter's first outfit on the rehearsal room wall. It showed her wearing a yellow-red fox-fur coat, a crimson scarf and a black macramé dress. Next to the drawing were several photographs of Marlene Dietrich, the Thirties star, famed for her cool beauty and husky voice.

Jon wasn't the only person to have Dietrich in mind for Mrs Coulter. When the adapter, Nicholas Wright, wrote the scene, he gave Mrs

Above: Dominic Leclerc (assistant staff director) and Nicholas Hytner (director) *(IK)*

Coulter an entrance and an opening line inspired by Dietrich's entrance in the movie *Witness for the Prosecution*, which he remembered seeing when he was twelve. It had struck him as unbelievably glamorous. In the film, Dietrich appears out of the shadows, where she has been listening to a conversation, huskily murmuring the line, "That won't be necessary."

Mrs Coulter was Pullman's favourite character after Lyra. "Mrs Coulter surprised me by turning out the way she did," he said, "She was always one step ahead of me." Patricia Hodge, who was playing the part, said, "We can't achieve precisely what is in people's heads when they read the book. What we *can* do is make these characters come to life."

They reached Mrs Coulter's first entrance, the encounter that changes Lyra's life, on the fourth day of rehearsal. In *Northern Lights*, Lyra meets Mrs Coulter in the Master's Drawing Room, where she sits next to her on a sofa, telling her everything about her half-wild life, and then sits next to her at dinner, and then carries on talking to her over coffee. At the end of the evening the idea is proposed to Lyra that she go to London to work as Mrs Coulter's assistant. Lyra has been totally captivated by Mrs Coulter before the offer is made, so it is no problem for Mrs Coulter to lead Lyra out of the cloistered security of Oxford into a world of adventure. "Lyra was intoxicated…" writes Pullman in *Northern Lights*, "What Mrs Coulter was saying seemed to be accompanied by… something disturbing but enticing… it was the smell of glamour."

Lord Asriel's first entrance, ten pages before Mrs Coulter's, would be a big theatrical number. The audience would hear the news that Lord Asriel was expected at Jordan College. They would hear a zeppelin drawing closer and the engine cutting out as it landed. Scholars would talk excitedly about Lord Asriel's imminent arrival. Lord Asriel's manservant, Thorold, would enter carrying his master's belongings, followed by Cawson, the steward of Jordan College, carrying more of Lord Asriel's belongings. Lord Asriel's daemon, the snow leopard, Stelmaria, would steal in, checking out the surroundings, and as the trumpet music built to its climax, Timothy Dalton would sweep in, wearing a long flowing trenchcoat and clutching military gloves, an action-man, briskly shaking hands with the fusty scholars. Late in rehearsals, this straightforward scene would be given a new twist (and added depth) by Lyra attempting to say hello to Lord Asriel and finding herself excluded and ignored.

If the audience was going to be made to wait and wait for Lord Asriel's fanfare entrance, Mrs Coulter's would take them by surprise: she appears out of the dark, an unexpected figure, cutting in sharply on a conversation. In *Play One* there would be no sofa in the drawing room, no civilised dinner party at which Lyra could sit next to Mrs Coulter and no coffee afterwards. Patricia Hodge had a twenty-five line scene in which to persuade Lyra to come and live with her in London and work as her personal assistant, an offer that Lyra has already rejected. It was a lot to do.

"There's not a lot to persuade her to go," said Patricia, when rehearsing the scene with Nick and Anna.

"The Arctic," said Nick.

"And Lord Asriel," said Anna.

"You completely seduce her," said Nick.

"No question of that," said Patricia, "There's just not a lot of space for her to do it. But that's my job."

Anna thought that Lyra would be persuaded. "It's incredibly exciting, It's like someone saying, 'Do you want to come to Disneyland?'"

The family drama between Mrs Coulter and Lyra and Lord Asriel had to be as convincing as possible. When Patricia had discussed playing the role with Nick, she had said that she could only do it if it was played for real. "Not *Gormenghast*" she said, referring to Mervyn Peake's fantastical novel. "Not *Gormenghast*," Nick agreed. "These

scenes have to be incredibly personalised," she said, "We've got to completely engage the audience in something they recognise. Other than the fantasy." The scenes between Mrs Coulter, Lyra and Lord Asriel were intense moments of domestic drama.

In *Northern Lights* Mrs Coulter is a mysterious figure whose actions keep surprising the reader. On stage, whatever Mrs Coulter does, there had to be a reason for doing it. "As an actor," Patricia said, "You ask yourself the question 'why' more times than you ever do in real life." An actor cannot think her character means two things at the same time. "Mrs Coulter can be perceived as ambiguous," she said, "But in playing her, I can't be. Because nobody is ever ambiguous to themselves. There should be a curious logic to everything she does."

If Mrs Coulter emerged from behind a pillar it would look sinister and would cast her as the villain. It was important that those members of the audience who hadn't read the books felt there was nothing suspicious about her. Patricia wanted to discuss the reason why Mrs Coulter planned to take Lyra to London.

Above: Patricia Hodge *(IK)*

"How long has this child-catching gone on?" she asked.

"A few years," suggested Nick.

"I'd have thought so," said Patricia. "It's become organised crime."

The adapter, Nicholas Wright, was watching the rehearsal. "She wants to take Lyra to London," he said, "and keep her where the Gobblers can't get her."

"It totally affects the way I come in," said Patricia, "It's not from behind a pillar."

"We're just going to have to sort that out," said Nick.

"Am I in an ante-room?"

"Possibly, yes. We have various options."

In a break in rehearsals, Patricia compared the experience to appearing in a musical where the scenes between songs are often extremely short. "You have to be a miniaturist. You have to bring a portrait to life in a small amount of time."

Mrs Coulter's daemon, the Golden Monkey, was one of the most-eye-catching in the rehearsal room, with orange hair, blue gobstopper eyes, and a lip that projected forward, like a conservatory extension. Who knew how younger members of the audience might react when they saw him? They might laugh, giggle or gasp. The monkey's puppeteer, Ben Wright, was learning to manipulate the two rods for the arms and the one for the neck. "Whether you like it or not," Nick said to Patricia, "the monkey's entrance is going to take everyone a second or two to get over."

Patricia wasn't worried about what the Golden Monkey would be doing. "The daemon is part of yourself," she said, "It shouldn't be at odds with you. So it's not for me to worry about. If it is doing something, I'm not noticing it." Her daemon had to be as instinctive to her as her own hands. "You don't look at your hands the whole time just because they are moving around."

A character might have only a short space of time on stage, but the theatre has a distinct advantage over the novel. It can tell the story in

Opposite: Ben Wright/the Golden Monkey *(IK)*

lots of ways at once. Mrs Coulter's character would be established by Patricia's performance, by her costume, by the lighting, by Anna's reaction as Lyra to her, and by the music. When Mrs Coulter makes her first entrance, Nick said to Patricia, "There'll almost certainly be a shimmer of music here."

"I like it," she said.

"Barbara Stanwyck-type music."

(Barbara Stanwyck was a Hollywood film actress of the 1940s, who played cool steely women.)

"God. A lot to live up to."

There would be no songs or dances in *His Dark Materials*, but the music would create mood, like a film score, and certain themes would be associated with characters. The composer Jonathan Dove said, "I will need to find things that will fight each other." He was sitting on the leather sofa in Nick's office on the fourth floor of the National, overlooking the Thames. They were discussing whether to have a Lyra theme and a Will theme and a Lyra instrument and a Will instrument. The audience first meets the twelve year old Lyra in Oxford.

"If there is a Lyra theme," Jonathan said, "That will be the bright chirpy version."

"That would be Lyra the urchin," said Nick, "as opposed to Lyra the lost soul."

The Subtle Knife would have a trumpet, the Gyptians would have a steady march, the music of people going on a quest, and the witches would have African drums. And what instrument would suit Mrs Coulter? "The great thing about Mrs Coulter," Nick said, "is that she is always totally unpinnable down." Jonathan's first idea was that Mrs Coulter should have "a different instrument every time". "It should always be fantastically attractive," said Nick. This idea changed to a seductive cello.

TWO OUT OF THREE of Pullman's titles in the English editions, *The Subtle Knife* and *The Amber Spyglass,* are props. In the American editions, where the first volume is titled *The Golden Compass*, all three are props. After Mrs Coulter and the Golden Monkey leave the study, the Master hands Lyra one of the three most important items in the plays. The alethiometer is the instrument with a range of symbols, and needles that move between them, that can answer questions. It acts in a similar way to the pictures on Tarot cards or the symbols in the *I*

Above: Steve Cartwright making the alethiometer prop *(CM)*

Ching. "There are dozens and dozens of ways of interrogating the universe," Pullman has said, "and the alethiometer is the one I made up for the book."

An alethiometer appeared in the rehearsal room in the first week. The props department travels all over the country visiting markets, fairs and shops for the props for *His Dark Materials*, but the alethiometer was found in a London antique shop in Camden Passage. It was a brass nautical compass that opened and closed and had maritime inscriptions on the top. (In *Northern Lights*, it says "it might have been a compass or something.") When it appeared on the stage manager's desk, Anna picked it up. "It's heavy," she said. (In *Northern Lights*, Lyra finds the alethiometer "surprisingly heavy".) Someone suggested to Anna that she put a mirror inside the lid so that she could check her make-up during the performance. "Yeah, as if Lyra's the sort of girl who worries about her lipstick." A fortnight before the show opened, this alethiometer was replaced with another, that looked less like a compass, and which opened by sliding apart, like an old-fashioned watch. It was based on an Islamic antique, found in a market in Kempton.

Anna knew from *Northern Lights* that the alethiometer had "three little knurled winding wheels" that made satisfying clicks. The details that absorb the reader do not carry across to a theatre audience. Pullman writes that Lyra found that "she could sink more and more readily into the calm state in which symbol-meanings clarified themselves." How was Anna going to draw a thousand people into the moment when she reads the alethiometer?

Anna wanted to know about the moment when the alethiometer actually begins to tell her something. "Will there be an effect?"

"There'll always be sound and music of some kind when this happens," said Nick.

In a meeting with Nick, Jonathan had said, "part of the music's role is to suggest the magical elements of the piece." The first idea that

Opposite: The rehearsal alethiometer *(CM)*

Jonathan suggested for the alethiometer music had been "a cascade of harpsichord and harp, possibly with a high piccolo or recorder, and a melody line that comes in as it spirals deeper and deeper." That idea changed to a glockenspiel, which gives a range of metallic sounds, without sounding tinkly and fairy tale.

There seemed to be two ways that Anna could read the alethiometer. Nick spelt out the choice. "You could put it on the floor, go into the trance, and go twist twist twist. Or we could get rid of the trance, and you go twist twist twist and look?"

Anna said, "I think it should almost have a life of its own. I go twist, twist, twist, and sit back, look at it, and it's really going. When I talk about what it's saying, that's part of the trance. She's still in it."

For Anna, the best advice about how to use the alethiometer came from Farder Coram in *Part One*, who tells Lyra not to yell at it like a drunken donkey-driver, but to treat it gently. "Now let your mind go free..." Farder Coram says, "and when the answer comes, reach down... and further down, till you find the level."

Above: Rehearsing the scene on board ship when Lyra reads the alethiometer *(IK)*

There had been a time during the first workshop, a year before, when Nick had tried an idea in which some of the actors would mime at the back of the stage what was happening inside the alethiometer. Nick told Anna that it was "one of the very few" ideas that Pullman had objected to. "Philip hated it, he *hated* it."

● ● ●

AS HER GUESTS are about to arrive for a party at her London home, Mrs Coulter asks Lyra to take off her bag. "It looks absurd to wear a shoulder bag in one's own home." Lyra refuses to take it off (it's where she keeps the alethiometer) and the Golden Monkey springs onto Pantalaimon, pinning him to the ground. One of the most riveting moments in the summer workshop had been when this happened. Lyra rolls on the floor in agony as – six feet away – Pantalaimon is throttled by the Golden Monkey. It was clear the dynamics between daemons and humans could be highly theatrical.

After the Golden Monkey's attack on her daemon, Lyra escapes from Mrs Coulter's home. The story becomes one about a young girl on the run. "London," says the stage direction, "Night and Fog." Two Tartar Guards attack Lyra, who is rescued by Tony Costa and his mate Ben. Tony tells Lyra the Gyptians are sailing to the Arctic to find the children who have been snatched by Gobblers. Lyra says, "I gotta come too."

In *Northern Lights*, the Gyptians wear leather jackets, spotted handkerchiefs and silver rings on their fingers. These are charming figures in a novel, but on stage they could look dangerously cosy. A novelist can take a few pages out to introduce new characters and situations, whereas once tension has been introduced in the theatre, the audience expects the temperature to keep rising. If a play loses the attention of the audience, it is doubly hard to regain it. An American playwright once compared the start of a play to an aeroplane taxi-ing onto the runway. No-one wants to sit on the tarmac for more than ten minutes. The plane has to take off, and once it has, you don't want to learn that it is shortly going to land and refuel. In the adaptation, it looked as if this was about to happen.

Nick was always looking for more 'aggro'. During the summer workshop he had liked the idea that the Gyptians were like armed guerrillas or French revolutionaries. "The stakes have to be really high." He thought the Gyptians might sing a sea shanty or a resistance song. "Like the freedom fighters in the Spanish Civil War. They're wild. They're tough." "Like Montenegran bandits," someone suggested. "Exactly."

During rehearsals the Gyptians were given an accent that was tough and unsentimental. The exact Fenlands accent chosen was north Norfolk. The dialect coach, Joan Washington, had sessions with the actors playing Gyptians. "I don't know why accents follow geographical features," she said, "but they tend to do so. The Fenland is cold, windy and flat. The wind's blowing in your face. It's an honest to God sound. Say what I mean. Take it or leave it." She gave them individual words as examples: forget is *forgit*; been is *bin*; new is *noo*; and she gave them a dozen sentences to practise. One of these went: "Tom caught an enormous cod." In a north Norfolk accent, nearly all the vowels in the sentence sound the same. *Taum caught an enaumous caud.*

The idea of a resistance song was dropped (as the composer Jonathan explained) because there no other songs in the show. The Gyptians disappear from the story in thirty pages' time, and it would have been disproportionate to give the one song in the show to a group of characters who fade from the narrative. Jonathan wrote a stirring march for the Gyptians that gives the sense of a group on a quest. Even before the audience see the Gyptians on board the ship or hear their flat windswept accents, they get a sense of the toughness and grittiness of these characters by hearing them scrape knives and sharpen weapons.

The Gyptians had given Pullman a chance to write about travelling by sea, and the slow changes in the sea and sky that reveal themselves on a long voyage ("it grew colder daily... one morning there was a different smell in the air"). This was an experience that Pullman had as a boy, travelling by ship to Africa and Australia, but the awesome beauty of the sea seemed impossible to catch on stage. The descriptions of Lyra's time on board the ship in *Northern Lights* are much closer in mood to the small boy's adventure in Edward Ardizzone's delightful illustrated book *Little Tim and the Brave Sea Captain*. Both Lyra and Little Tim make friends on board ship and discover that the best way to get along is to make yourself useful. The mood is quite different for this scene in the play. There's more aggro: the Gyptians are surly, brooding figures, most of whom are actively hostile to Lyra.

When he was writing the adaptation, Nicholas Wright had always imagined a ship would come into view, rather as had happened in a production he had seen of *Treasure Island.* In the early designs Giles had experimented with the deck of a ship and flags, barrels and crates. The fate of the ship hung on how far it could meet the main principles of the production: keeping everything moving and keeping Lyra in peril.

Only two things happen on board the ship: Lyra manages to read the alethiometer for the first time and she is spotted by spyflies working for Mrs Coulter. Neither of these events is big enough in itself – or sufficiently connected to Lyra's voyage – to warrant a big ship scene. When he was directing one of the workshops, Nick had spelt out the precise threat Mrs Coulter's spyflies posed to the Gyptians. "If they have found us, she knows where we are. So, more peril. The point about the flies is that they're spies, not that they're lethal." The other disadvantage with the ship was that this was about a journey from England to Trollesund, the ship provides the journey, but not the contrast between the two places.

They discussed this sequence at Giles' studio in Kilburn. "This is the really hard bit," said Giles, "How do we get off the ship?" Nick said, "In an ideal world, the atmosphere that you want to get from the ship is, you're in the north now, you've hit the snows and the wide open spaces." There were three separate scenes in this section: getting on the ship; the time on the ship leading to the arrival at Trollesund ("Land ahoy!"); and landing at Trollesund and getting off the ship. Which scene was the big visual one?

The discussions between Giles and Nick boiled down to a simple fact: a boat was a boat. Everyone knew what it was like on a boat. Giles and Nick wanted the contrast between the night-time streets of London and the chilly expanse of the North. Giles' solution was to turn the ship scene into an interior one, inside the rusty old hulk, so that when the shout comes ("Land ahoy!"), Lyra and the Gyptians would climb up a ladder and see a spectacular new landscape. The big moment in the sequence would be the arrival at the northern seaport of Trollesund. It is here that Lyra meets a Texan aeronaut called Lee Scoresby, a snow goose called Kaisa and a bear called Iorek. This unlikely bunch join together to go on a mission to find Roger and the other children who have been abducted by the Gobblers.

It feels a bit like a famous Western (on the one hand) and a famous musical (on the other). The famous Western was *The Magnificent Seven*, starring Steve McQueen and Yul Brynner, in which a Mexican village is harrassed by bandits, and the villagers hire seven guys to defend them. In *His Dark Materials* the threatened Mexican village becomes the children abducted by the Gobblers, and Anna and Sam and the others are Steve McQueen, Yul Brynner, etc. The connection is not accidental. "*The Magnificent Seven* has been with me for a very long time," Pullman once said, "since my boyhood." The famous musical is *The Wizard of Oz*, where Dorothy links up with the Cowardly Lion, the Straw Man and the Tin Man on her journey down the yellow brick road.

This created a challenge for Nick. The way the story unfolds in *Northern Lights*, Lyra spends time in Oxford, then in London, and then with the Gyptians, before she sails with them to the North, where she recruits her own Magnificent Seven. The business of Lyra going round gathering enough people for the task ahead should happen at the beginning of the story, on pages five to twenty of a script, and not – as was about to happen here – on pages forty to sixty. For the play to work, Lyra had to stay in constant peril. She was the audience's way into the story and she had to be in danger. The Church had to be be after her; Mrs Coulter had to be after her; and there had to be the ever-present threat of Tartars or Gobblers seizing her at any moment and packing her off to Bolvangar, where terrible things were rumoured to happen.

"What I've always thought," said Nick, at one of the pre-production meetings, "is you've just got the story cooking, and then there's this 'time out', meeting some very nice, very boring Gyptians, a bear with a drink problem, and a Texan with a balloon. It's always going to be a hurdle. If it's tense enough at this point, we can take a breather. I can see this is always going to annoy me, because it doesn't pick up again until she's in Bolvangar. The quest structure gives you time to meet new friends and new enemies. The problem is that we forget the enemies."

● ● ●

Chapter Four

"I would love to work here. It looks much more fun than writing."
Philip Pullman

PULLMAN'S THREE BOOKS appeared over a period of seven years, and each one was self-contained and built to its own climax. In turning the three books into two plays, one of the biggest challenges that Nicholas Wright faced was deciding where to put the middle. There would be a moment when the ending to *Northern Lights* would have to dovetail with the opening of *The Subtle Knife*. The first book takes place in Lyra's world, and the reader doesn't realise that it is not happening in ours, it simply appears that Lyra's world has some strange and unusual aspects. "When you start the second book," said Nicholas Wright, "You think, oh my God, that wasn't our world where the first book was happening, it was a completely different world, and *now* we're in our world." In *The Subtle Knife* the reader doesn't follow

Lyra's story but Will's. This isn't the kind of shift that can be made in a stage version. "It doesn't work so well if, half way through the second half of the play, you stop telling Lyra's story," said Wright, "and start telling Will's. If you set off with Lyra's story you want to continue on that, and Will's story has to be fed into it in a way which feels organic." The whole production of *His Dark Materials* would depend on the skill of the transitions, and the transition between the last page of *Northern Lights* and the first page of *The Subtle Knife* was the biggest of all.

"This is going to be hopeless," said Nick. His face lengthened, one hand covered his forehead and his eyelids lowered. Suggestions were obviously not welcome. He had warned the company at the start of that day's rehearsal that this was easily the most complex sequence in the whole of *Part One*. It was going to be "slow and fiddly". The goal with an action sequence is clear visual storytelling. The problem was that Nick had half a dozen stories to tell.

He ran the scene through in his head. A model of the Olivier theatre sat in one corner of the rehearsal room, showing the drum revolve, the rim revolve, and the various levels at which the machinery could stop on its sixty foot journey up and down. Nick had no need to look at the model: he had it inside his head.

In effect, the scene was the stage version of the final chapter of *Northern Lights*. In Chapter 23, Lyra and Pantalaimon cross the snowbridge, find Lord Asriel, discover what he is going to do to Lyra's best friend Roger, try and rescue Roger, and run away. There is a nuclear explosion, Roger dies, Mrs Coulter rejects Lord Asriel's invitation to walk through the Aurora Borealis, Lord Asriel walks through to another world and – minutes later – so do Lyra and Pantalaimon. End of *Northern Lights*.

At the climax of all this frenetic activity there was one small problem. Roger's dead body was still on stage. How were they going to get Russell Tovey, who was playing Roger, and had only recently collapsed to the ground and died, off the stage? Nick said, "The only

Opposite: Russell Tovey *(IK)*

thing, Russell that you can do, the only available thing is crawl off with the snowbridge." Seconds later, he said, "Actually there is an alternative…" Roger dies *on* the snowbridge, and when it circles off, so does he.

After the explosion, Timothy Dalton would turn away from the audience and walk through the Aurora Borealis. "We will make sure this is good to look at," said Nick. It was only at the Technical, when the video arrived, that the actors would have any idea what a hole in the Aurora Borealis would look like. So many elements would arrive at that late stage, that the cast would not fully understand what they were doing till then. "It can't really happen till we get it on stage," said Patricia Hodge, "because there are so many other influences that will be telling the story to us as much as to the audience."

The play was about to go into Will's world, but the difference from the book was that the story would stay with Lyra. She remains in peril. The Church knows Lyra is bad, but doesn't know what her secret name is till the beginning of *Part Two*. Nick said, "We have to send Lyra through the Aurora with the Church going, 'We're going to get you'. They know Lyra's the enemy. But they don't know which enemy. That gives us somewhere to go."

It was only at the read-through, two weeks before the first day of rehearsal, that Nick sensed how this fusing of the first book and the second book would work. Nearly all the cast had assembled in a long room, where they sat at a conference table, with bottles of mineral water and copies of the scripts in front of each place. After that read-through, Nick said, "It was the first time I didn't think the play should end here. That's always going to be the test. It's partly about what you cut to after the snowbridge." Where do you pick up the story once Lyra has gone through the Aurora Borealis? Nick's answer was, "Cut to the witches. We have to find her. She's in peril."

● ● ●

THREE OF THE WITCHES were going to be played by men.

"Are you sure you're going to be a witch?" an actress asked one of the actors at the first witches' rehearsal.

"My name is up on the board," he said, "Why else have I been called?"

"You'd better get some tits," she said.

The associate director, Aletta Collins, asked the actors – male and female – to stand in a circle and close their eyes. "It's the dead of night," she said, "You're up in the dark skies, and you're flying, the wind is rushing past you, the warm gentle wind through the dark night sky; it's exhilarating…"

A soundtrack of wind played in the background. "The wind is blowing through your hair," said Aletta, "and you're drinking it in, and you're picking up speed, and the first star comes into sight…"

Aletta's script for *His Dark Materials* was sitting on a table at the back of the rehearsal room. On the script she had written half a dozen notes: "the sky. the stars. the wind. the lover. the sun. eternity." These were the ideas she wanted to get across. "And the star brushes past,"

Above: Dominic Cooper and Anna Maxwell Martin *(IK)*

she said, as the wind on the soundtrack continued to blow, "You feel the tingle as it brushes you, and with each touch you feel a little more alive and you're flying into the Milky Way, and everywhere around you is a bed of stars. This is where you come from…"

The actors swayed gently in the middle of Rehearsal Room One. In *Northern Lights*, Serafina Pekkala, the Queen of the Lapland witches says, "A witch would no sooner give up flying than give up breathing. To fly is to be perfectly ourselves." If someone had walked in to rehearsals at that moment they would have had no idea that the circle of actors could fly as easily as they could breathe.

"You're flying out, out, out," said Aletta, "into a heavy sky in the distance, and that star in the distance, coming towards you, it's the face of your first mortal lover…" The actors' hands stretched out, their feet moved a few steps forward, a few steps sideways.

Above: Niamh Cusack *(IK)*

In the stage version, none of the witches would be up in the air. In a pre-production meeting, Nick had said, "I really don't want to get into harnesses and wires." It takes a whole day of technical rehearsals to fix the flying for a show like *Peter Pan*. There would be very few days for technical rehearsals. They had none to spare for harnesses and wires.

"And as the star comes closer," said Aletta, "catch the star – but his face is changing, he's growing old before your eyes, and you're having to pass him, because you have to fly on…" The actors were learning to fly without their feet ever leaving the ground.

"And you're flying past, another lover, another son," said Aletta, "You're having to fly past them, and they're growing old, and crumbling…" The way the actors were going to fly was simply through movement. In one exercise they would move through heavy gaseous air, as if a witch moved through air the way a person moved through water. In another exercise they would practise being blown back by gusts of wind. In a third they would use their cloud-pines like javelins or harpoons that would skewer the ground as they landed. The very first exercise was to learn to think and feel like witches.

"And there's another star and it's your son, and he's growing old too. And you're not changing," said Aletta, taking them deeper and deeper into other galaxies, taking them to places where the veils between the worlds are thin and the witches hear the whispers of immortal beings, "You're going forward, forward, up into a darker sky…"

For the actors (three of them male) standing and swaying in the rehearsal room, it was going to be a long journey.

●●●

ON THE FIRST MORNING of rehearsal, when the cast had read *Part One*, Nick passed a note to one of the actors, Stephen Greif, saying "would you do him as Donald Rumsfeld". Stephen pulled a thoughtful face as he recalled the American Defence Secretary's voice, and minutes later he read the first of the President of the Consistorial Court's lines in a light steely voice. As he did so, Nick, the director, looked at Nick, the adapter, and they grinned at one another. The idea had been in Nick Hytner's mind for weeks. At the design meeting in Kilburn he had said, "I'm thinking of doing the President as Donald Rumsfeld. What do you think?" Everyone smiled. "Well, we'll try it."

The Church is the most powerful institution in Lyra's world and the President of the Consistorial Court is its most powerful representative. In the book, the President's name is MacPhail. Stephen had been planning to play him as a Scot – he was thinking of the tough Labour politician John Reid. When Nick suggested Rumsfeld, Stephen got hold of the BBC interview with David Dimbleby, to learn the Defence Secretary's rhythms and accent.

Above: Stephen Greif *(IK)*

One of the first major changes that the plays make to the novels is that the Church is on Lyra's case from the start. Fra Pavel, an emissary from Geneva, has been regularly visiting Jordan College to check on her progress. The Church emerges in the books and the plays as thoroughly unpleasant. There are hints of Communist Russia and Nazi Germany. "It's pretty aggressive," Nick said about Pullman's treatment of the Church, "It means to offend. The Church, we know, has been responsible for a lot of harm. So there's no need to soften it. He's not writing about sweet gay bishops from New Hampshire."

When Lyra leaves her world – the Church's world – and goes through to another one, the Church has to find a way to track her down. It's this that leads to the development of a bomb that could still kill Lyra in a parallel universe. By going through the Aurora, Lyra also meets Will.

Up to this point, Dominic, who plays Will, has had scenes as the grown-up Will, sitting on the bench in the Botanic Garden, and has played a Tartar Guard killed by an arrow, and an armoured bear. From now on, he plays twelve-year-old Will. "We're not being made to play an age," he said, "Doing child acting is completely the wrong way to go." It was the things the characters do that revealed their age. "We would never in a million years do what they do. They jump through a window they've just made in the air, through to another universe. They're fearless."

In twenty pages' time he will be fighting for the Subtle Knife. To win the knife, Dominic met up with Terry King, the fight director, who would choreograph his struggle with Ben Wright, playing Tullio. As they rehearsed, Terry gave a running commentary. "Spin him round! Bite, bite, bite! Push, push, push! Into the strangle! Into the poke in the eye!"

The way to poke someone in the eye (evidently) was to jab the finger behind the other's person's head. The finger has to go beyond the profile of that person's face, but mustn't stay there; the effect comes from pulling it rapidly away. "It bounces away." said Terry,

"Kerchunk! and it bounces away. It's the speed and intention of it."
Dominic and Ben knew the poke in the eye was working when Terry
said, "Okay, I buy that."

After the poke in the eye, there was the knee in the groin and the
desperate lurch towards the knife, with Ben pulling Dominic back, and
Dominic's hand stretching forward, until he grabs the knife and Ben
pulls away. As Nick explained it, "The place we've decided to end *Part
One* is Will becoming the bearer of the knife. Oh my God. It's *Paradise
Lost.* It's the war on God."

● ● ●

BY THE FOURTH WEEK they had rehearsed the whole of *Part One*
and Nick needed to know how long it would run. It could only be three
hours including a 20-minute interval. A family show needs to finish by
10.30pm. People have to get home. There are last trains to catch. Any
later, and during the last ten minutes of the show, members of the
audience would start getting up and leaving.

Nick told the cast, "I've never done this before. Generally, I don't do
a run-through till much later. But we have so few previews that we
can't make any changes then to the plays themselves. I know we have
only rehearsed some of the scenes for half an hour, and I'd be amazed
if they were good."

Nick wanted to ensure there were no delays. Actors were advised to
carry their scripts if they were unsure of the lines. "I'll probably shout
what happens next. I'll probably interrupt in the middle of a scene and
say, 'Come on Gyptians, you're on next.'"

The first act started with one of the stage managers going *ding,
ding, ding, ding, ding, ding, ding, ding, ding, ding, ding.* It was
midnight in the Botanic Garden. After fifteen minutes, Lyra had met
Lord Asriel, after 27 minutes she had met Mrs Coulter, after 30
minutes she had received the alethiometer, after 53 minutes she had

teamed up with the Gyptians, after 60 minutes she had met Iorek, after 75 minutes, she was in Bolvangar, after 81 minutes she had seen the severed daemons, after 85 minutes she discovered who her father was (Lord Asriel), after 90 minutes she discovered who her mother was (Mrs Coulter), and after 91 minutes she was whisked away by Serafina Pekkala.

During the break there was a mood of quiet concentration. Two actors practised the bear-fight. Two others ran lines from their library scene. Another lifted his shirt and sprayed himself with deodorant. A stage manager moved a rack of bears' heads across the room. One actor read *Time Out*. Another stood near the coffee machine and said that the last hour and a half had been terrifying. Patricia said, "It's the most off-the-wall show I've ever seen." Sam ate a home-made sandwich out of silver foil. Anna drank herbal tea and sent a text message. Nick and the other Nick (the adapter) discussed the plot. The costume designer, Jon, and his assistant, Emma, discussed the strap on Anna's costume for Lyra. The set designer, Giles, flicked through pictures of the set and made notes on a yellow legal pad. A video camera was recording the entire morning so that Jonathan could take it home, play it, and write music to the exact length.

"Okay," said the stage manager, after the twenty-minute break, "Can we settle down please." A minute later, the stage manager said, "Can we stand by please?" Anna put the bag over her shoulder with the alethiometer in it and sat on the bench next to Dominic. The pine marten version of Pantalaimon had been placed next to her. Behind Anna and Dominic, several actors crouched in a circle of red tape, which represented the balloon. The stage manager said, "And..." and another stage manager, nodded to the actors, "Okay..."

As soon as Anna finished her scene on the bench in the Botanic Garden, she joined the others inside the red tape. After seven minutes Lyra had been captured and taken to Iofur Raknison, after fourteen minutes Iofur was fighting Iorek, after seventeen minutes Lyra had met up again with Lord Asriel, after 33 minutes Roger was dead, after 34 minutes Lord Asriel set off through the Aurora to kill the Authority and Lyra and Pan followed, after 37 minutes the witches convened, after 42 minutes Lyra met Will in Cittàgazze, after 81 minutes Giacomo Paradisi shows Will how to use the knife, after 84 minutes Will has cut a hole between universes, and after 86 minutes he has learnt how to stitch the hole up again. After 88 minutes, the angels were flying north to join Lord Asriel in the fight against the Authority.

"We have a little additional thing to tag on to this," Nick said, "with Mrs Coulter and Lord Asriel and the President coming on. The good news is that, excluding the break, it lasted about three hours. There will be little snips and alterations to tease out the story. We're not looking for huge cuts, but we are looking for 20 minutes, maybe 25. We're just going to make sure the whole style of playing keeps rolling on. That it's constantly on a roll. Because that's when it works best."

While the minutes had ticked away on the clock above the coffee machine, another problem was staring Nick in the face. After lunch he shared the news with the cast. He was blunt about it. The daemons weren't working.

● ● ●

FROM THE FIRST WEEK'S rehearsal it had been clear that daemons worked when they moved slowly, moved slightly, or moved, paused and moved. The two things that didn't work were rapid irregular movements or no movement at all. A daemon looked particularly exposed when it was held at arm's length and didn't move. At those moments, the actors might have been exhibiting expensive vases at a Sotheby's auction. It was easy enough to imagine a small daemon was alive when it was cupped or cosseted; but even this could be difficult for an actor to sustain when he or she had some other piece of stage business to do. When an actor had a prop in one hand, the daemon in the other hand usually went dead. It could be maddening to watch: one moment you had invested imaginatively in the life of something that was purely a theatrical conceit, and in the next moment, the character had vanished, there was nothing there, except for a lifeless puppet. It was the birds, especially the large ones like the owl, the vulture and the macaw, that were the quickest to lose their sense of life.

Nick's bleak announcement that the daemons weren't working prompted nervous banter in the queue at the canteen. One cast member asked, "Where did your puppet train?" "The puppets are fine," another said, "We just need to get some new actors." It was the first time in the canteen I had heard the cast discussing how rehearsals were going and what should be done about them. One phrase was repeated: "You know, there's only five weeks."

What if the daemons didn't work (or, for that matter, the bears, the witches or the Gallivespians)? What if a daemon was simply a literary idea and not a theatrical one. Other theatre directors had read the books and decided they were impossible to stage. Perhaps they were

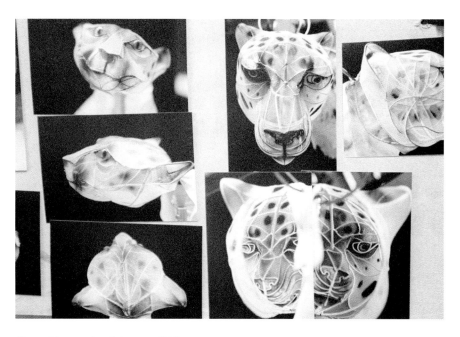

Above: Photographs of daemons *(CM)*

right. When he wrote about daemons Pullman didn't have to keep them alive in every paragraph; he could mention them whenever he wanted. Once the daemons had appeared on stage, once the illusion had been introduced, they had to be kept alive, the illusion had to be maintained.

A worrying sign in the rehearsal room (after the bleak announcement) was the sight of Nick chewing gum. I had seen him chewing gum before. In the video about the making of *Miss Saigon*, the 1989 blockbuster musical Nick had directed when in his early thirties, there is footage of him directing the show (he had short brown hair and large-rimmed glasses). The tension in those rehearsals was evident from the way he was chewing gum. He was doing it again in Rehearsal Room One; he was giving the gum a real pounding.

It was as if the task of condensing the 1300 pages of the three novels into two plays (a task Nick had once referred to in a workshop as "pouring a petrol station into a pint pot") had been so demanding, and the technical complexities involved in finding a way of staging a hundred scenes so intricate, that the question of the daemons (and, for that matter, the bears, the witches and the Gallivespians) had been neglected. Each of these groups would need – as the phrase went – their own physical language. They were five weeks' away from opening (as everyone kept saying) and a convincing language had yet to be found for any of these groups. For the first time, I thought, the whole thing might not work.

At moments like these, when a production looks in trouble, the director or producer (and Nick was both) tends to tighten his/her control over every aspect of the production, sack people and raise his voice. Nick went the other way. He said, "The thing I think I'm really learning on this production is delegation." He was going to hand the whole problem of the daemons (and, for that matter, the bears, the witches and the Gallivespians) over to Aletta, his associate director,

Opposite: Brewyeen Rowland (ASM) and Kerry McDevitt (DSM) *(IK)*

and to the staff director, Matt Wilde, the assistant staff director, Dominic Leclerc, and the fight director, Terry King.

Inside Rehearsal Room One, Nick would get on with the business of staging each of the scenes. Outside Rehearsal Room One, other highly specialised rehearsals took place. It was possible to see just how many activities were going on at once from the lengthy call sheets posted by the rehearsal room door. The schedule would announce which actors needed to be available to rehearse 'Lord Asriel's fortress', which were doing 'daemon work', which had a 'bear fight' to go to, which had 'voice work', and which had wig and costume fittings. In 'daemon work' the actors would have individual rehearsal calls to work with Aletta, Matt or Dominic on the particular characteristics of their daemons. These rehearsals would also be attended by David or Yvonne, two of the puppet-makers, who were looking for new ways to make the daemons more flexible.

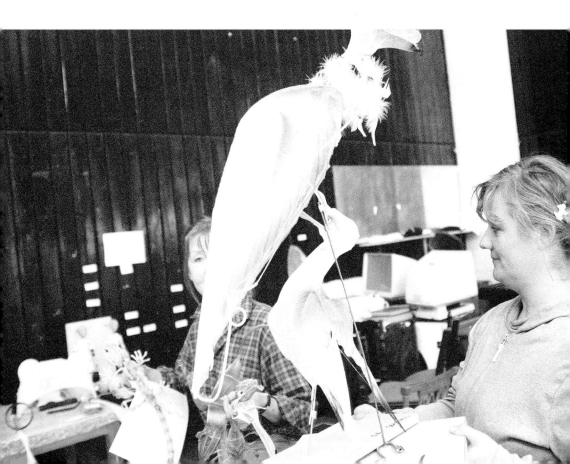

The collaboration between various departments intensified. The puppet department was working with the actors, the directors and the costume-makers, to find ways of placing the daemons on the bodies, ways of making slits and gaps in the costumes to conceal part of the daemons, ways of attaching magnets and mounts to the costumes to hold the the daemons, and ways of threading fine string from the puppets through the costumes and onto a ring on the hand of an actor, so that he could twitch the beak or flutter the wings of his daemon bird. The nature of the daemons was changing too: sometimes it was only necessary to create the head and the tail, as the body could be concealed within the clothing. Video tapes began to show up in rehearsals: David Attenborough's *Life of Birds, Toy Story 2* and a documentary about wolves. The main half dozen daemons, the ones operated by puppeteers, were Lyra's Pantalaimon, Mrs Coulter's Golden Monkey, Lord Asriel's snow leopard, Stelmaria, Roger's Salcilia, Lee Scoresby's hare Hester and Serafina Pekkala's snow goose, Kaisa. In the 'daemon work' rehearsals for these main daemons, every move they made in a scene was worked out and marked down. The new phrase for all this activity was 'physical underscore'.

Pantalaimon was changing. A small handle had been attached to the scruff of his neck, which gave Sam far more movement. Sam also used his other hand to hold Pantalaimon's tail, which he would swish from side to side. Sam was keeping Pantalaimon closer to the ground, the movements were slower, and when Pantalaimon was scared, he would turn back to Lyra and nestle between her feet. His colour had changed too as the puppet-department repainted his coat from a milky grey to a russet red. Pullman's new book, *Lyra's Oxford*, had just been published and on the second page he described Pantalaimon as "lazily grooming his red-gold fur".

If Sam had been sent a job description (before he signed his contract) it might have read: you will be wearing a black outfit with a

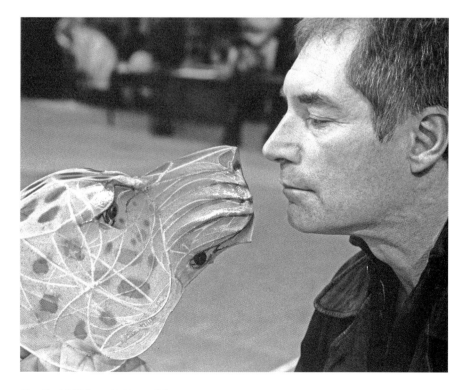

Top: Tim McMullan with Hester *(IK)*

Above: Timothy Dalton with Stelmaria *(IK)*

black mask. You will hold the character that you are playing in your hand. The character you are holding will be part of Lyra's character and will change shape, sometimes in the middle of a scene, sometimes between scenes. Sometimes Lyra will hold the character that you play and you will stand next to her or you will disappear from the scene entirely. Sometimes your character will be inside her handbag. Your job across the six hour story will be to make the audience care desperately about a creature that either you are holding or not holding in whatever shape or size it happens to be.

• • •

Above: Jonathan Dove (composer) *(IK)*
Opposite: Jon Morrell's notebook *(CM)*

AFTER SIX WEEKS, Philip Pullman made his next appearance in the rehearsal room. Jonathan had installed a piano and two keyboards and was feeding music into the action. The scene Pullman was watching was given extra urgency by 'hurry' music, as Jonathan played rapid little sequences when Lyra and Pantalaimon are on the run, and extra danger by 'panic' music, as he thumped out low pounding chords when they are attacked.

The sense of hurry and danger within the rehearsal room increased markedly when the fire alarm went off. The stage manager told everyone in the room to leave the building as quickly as possible. In the corridors outside, the *Dark Materials* actors joined the actors who had been rehearsing *Mourning Becomes Electra* in the room next door. The star of the current hit movie *Calendar Girls*, Helen Mirren, was walking in front. "Keep together please!" shouted the stage manager, as people spread out across the foyer, past the bookshop, onto the cobbled embankment overlooking the Thames.

On the embankment, a middle-aged man was sitting on a bench reading the paper. Within a couple of minutes he had been surrounded by several hundred people. There were a number of well-known actors, some of whom had been in major Hollywood movies, standing yards away from him. With British cool, he refused to look up from his paper.

A man in a yellow jacket bearing the words 'Incident Officer' organised National Theatre employees into groups. 'Marketing' stood in one place, 'Box Office' in another, 'Accounts' in another. At this hour of the morning, none of the actors was in costume. It was the non-actors who were dressed up: the kitchen staff wore white, the cleaners wore blue shirts with red collars, and security wore black.

It was hard to imagine the grey concrete tiers of the National catching fire. Philip Pullman chatted to Helen Mirren. Anna and Dominic played pat-a-cake. Emma, the costume assistant, had brought her folder of costume designs out with her (presumably, the most precious thing in the building). The executive director, Nick Starr, had a bunch of newspaper cuttings under his arm and was checking a text message on his phone. Big articles about *His Dark Materials* had just appeared in *The Daily Telegraph* and the *Observer*. After each piece was published, the box office takings had shot up. By that morning ticket sales for the two plays had reached an all time box office record for the National, and the marketing director, Chris Harper, was confident that by the opening night they would almost have sold out. Minutes later, all the employees, some of whom had never seen each other before, filed back into the building through the stage door. It had been a fire practice.

As he watched rehearsals, Pullman played with one of the pocket-sized Gallivespians on his knees. In a break in rehearsals, he went over to look at the daemons at the back of the room. He moved quietly along the trestle tables, his hands cupped behind his back, like the head teacher judging the art prize. He was asked if he would like to see the workshops.

He went through a door marked 'paint frame'. In front were half a dozen polystyrene blocks with steel prongs. The scene makers were carving it into the shapes of trees. In the corner were branches, twigs and leaves that would be added later. At the far end of the room were the green exterior walls of Jordan College. On the other side of the wall, a scenic artist was stencilling a pattern of lizards on the interior of the Master's study.

On the back wall was a large elevator – known as a 'working platform' – that could move up and down and left and right. A vast orange silk backdrop hung on the wall. Was this part of *His Dark Materials*? The silk had been dyed a golden brown and painted with chestnut and cerise. On the platform, Hilary Vernon-Smith was painting it to look like horrible old tarpaulin. It had to be silk because it had to be folded away. This would be the tarpaulin with the letters G.O.B., standing for the General Oblation Board, the organisation that was secretly abducting children and taking them to Bolvangar. The

Above: Philip Pullman *(IK)*

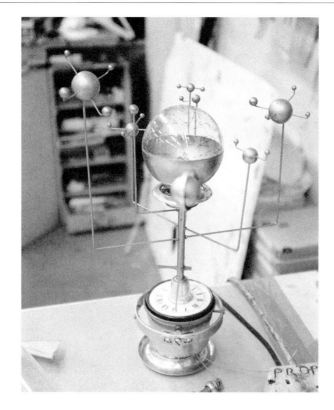

tarpaulin would hang on the dockside, next to the bleak collection point, where the children caught by the Gobblers assembled for their trip to the north.

In the props workshop next door to the paintframe, the props maker Terri Anderson was working on the panel for the machine that separates the daemon from the child. "Is it going to fizz and bang?" Pullman asked. Not exactly. The panel of dials had red cones that lit up. On her workbench, Terri had a photocopy of a picture of the nuclear reactor at Berkeley, California. Pullman looked at the picture. "Seems about right."

Outside the props workshop, Pullman examined some luxury beach huts from Holland. The designer Giles had wanted these as shelters for the people who sit and wait in the suburbs of the dead. Pullman admired the wicker frame, the woodwork and the adjustable canvas roof. The stage manager walked past and said, "They've been cut." The

Above: Props workshop *(CM)*

designer had liked the idea but the director hadn't. The three beach huts shared corridor space with stacks of jugs, vases, sculptures and a forklift elevator. Pullman studied the way the hut's little sidetable folded out for drinks. A member of the backstage crew walked past and ticked him off. "I hope the designer knows you're touching those." Pullman lifted both hands away with an air of gentle apology.

At the end of drum road was a small workshop, the size of a caravan. Inside several women were at work. One of them, Vicky, had the *EyeWitness Book of Lizards* open on the page showing an iguana. She was painting a puppet the colours of the iguana. Another, Lara, was working on a wire head small enough to fit into the palm of her hand. The man who created the idea of daemons had found the room at the very back of the theatre where the daemons were made.

Pullman looked at the head Lara was making for one of the rodent daemons. Pictures of daemons were pinned on the wall above her table next to anatomical pictures of the human body. Lara demonstrated how she bent the copper-plated wires into shape. Pullman asked about the gauze. Lara explained that it was powernet, an industrial fabric which stretches easily without tearing. "It's very forgiving."

Bears' heads hung on the wall. Pullman took one down and inspected the wire frame inside. "Is it welded or soldered?" (Both.) "How many are there?" (Sixteen.) "How many daemons are there?" (About fifty.) He wanted to know what wood had been used for the Gallivespians. (Limewood.) He picked up the remains of the large lump of this blonde wood, which is soft enough to carve, but retains its strength. He said he was using tulipwood for the head of the rocking horse he was making.

As he said goodbye, he said, with evident sincerity, "I would love to work here. It looks much more fun than writing."

● ● ●

Chapter Five

"Say something."
Pantalaimon

BY THE FRIDAY AFTERNOON of the tenth week, the late-November weather had turned dark and wet. The few windows in Rehearsal Room One were pitch black. As the cast ran *Part Two* the actors who were not in scenes sat round the edges on sofas, tables, crates and chairs, in between telescopes, wireless sets, rifles, daemons, cliffghasts, bears' heads and cups of chocolatl.

At the end of the run, the cast formed a semi-circle and Nick gave some notes. Nearly all were about telling the story with more clarity: someone needed to 'ping' this moment or 'place' that word, this detail was getting lost, that line couldn't be heard. After half an hour of notes, Nick made a separate point. He said that a single question had given him the biggest pause for thought when he was considering a stage version of *His Dark Materials*.

He said the conventional wisdom was that when a director staged a big show in the Olivier with a female lead, the woman playing the part had to be in her thirties or older, and had to have a big commanding voice, even a hectoring one, that could hold the stage. It was this single worry that had made him think longest and hardest about whether or not to do two plays in the Olivier which featured a twelve-year-old as the central character. Nick said that, thanks to Anna, this simply hadn't been a worry. He couldn't imagine doing this production with anyone else. The cast applauded, Anna pulled an 'aw-shucks' face, and Nick added, "She's also the bossiest actress I've ever worked with." Anna let out one of her familiar gutsy cackles.

There would be no rehearsals on Saturday (for once), so that evening the Green Room bar was packed with the company. Anna and Dominic were there, and Aletta was sitting at a table with a daemon on

it (well, he deserved a drink too). At one of the tables, Danny Sapani, who plays Iorek, was reflecting on the ten weeks of rehearsal. When he was cast as Iorek, he had no idea how he was going to play a bear. Whenever he is cast in television programmes (*Holby City, The Bill, Between The Lines*, etc.) he is asked to play characters who are as close as possible to what he is actually like. Danny is a big bloke, he's in his thirties and he's black. Essentially, on TV, he is hired to play himself. In theatre, the opposite was the case.

All he had been given in rehearsals was a bear's mask, which he held in one hand, a claw he held in the other, and a white hoop that linked the two. Aletta had said the witches were going to be creatures of the sky and the bears earth-bound. They would be lumbering figures that moved in a pack: when one turned his head, they all turned their heads. In the first few weeks, Danny had used the mask

Above: Danny Sapani *(IK)*

and claw as props, as he imagined he would communicate with the audience through his own face. He used the mask and claw, he said, "as a sword and a shield'.

Halfway through rehearsals, Aletta told him that the mask would "magnify Iorek's feelings." That piece of advice proved a turning-point for Danny. He used the bear's mask – like the masks in Ancient Greek plays – as his main means of expression. It's part of the alchemy of theatre that inanimate objects can become expressive. Danny had an advantage over actors in Greek drama in that he had a claw he could use too. He didn't make his face blank, but projected all his thoughts through the bear's head – a white mask, with wire outlines, black eye sockets and a black nose. His grip for the mask was a bar like a handlebar. The other actors always addressed the mask rather than Danny's face. He also watched videos of polar bears and discovered that, when they fight, they stand up, clutch hold of each other, claw at each other and even stamp on one another's feet. When Danny reaches the palace at Svalbard and the usurping king, Iofur Raknison, challenges him to single combat, Danny clutches Iofur, claws Iofur and even stamps on the feet of his rival.

Above: Sheila Slaymaker knotting hair onto a balaclava, for a bear's wig *(CM)*

At the start of the bear rehearsals, the idea had been to make the bears fairly comical, a motley bunch from the North, complaining in Yorkshire accents about the latest injustices perpetrated by Iofur Raknison. This didn't work. "The more I rehearse this play," Nick said, "the more I think it works best whenever we take the scenes seriously." When Philip Pullman heard that rehearsals had moved from presenting the bears as comic figures to presenting them seriously, he said the same process had taken place in the screenplay, which had started out using the bears as light relief. That section of the screenplay was now being rewritten. It was the same lesson Pullman had learnt when writing school plays: the way to appeal to children and adults at the same time was to take the story seriously. Pullman murmured something, very lightly, about knowing what he had been doing.

On the Saturday morning, while the actors were enjoying a day off, and England were winning the Rugby World Cup, scenic artists were backstage painting the inside of the droom. In the Olivier the final two performances of *His Girl Friday* were taking place that afternoon and evening. The evening performance would finish at 10.30pm, and from that moment on, every hour in the Olivier theatre over the next four weeks had been accounted for by the *His Dark Materials* production team.

Each Thursday lunchtime the production manager, Sacha Milroy, had chaired a production meeting at which representatives from all the departments discussed the progress they had made and raised any matters they needed to discuss with others. The tenth Thursday lunchtime had been the last production meeting. At the beginning, Sacha handed out about thirty copies of a four-page document titled 'Production Schedule: Draft 3 – *His Dark Materials*' which listed, in very small type, the schedule as it would run from that Saturday morning through to the press night.

There was a column called 'crew call', which spelt out exactly who would be needed and when. On Saturday night, as soon as *His Girl*

Friday had finished, the call for the crew would be: '14-16 Stage, 3 Flys, 6LX and 2 Sound'; that is, fourteen to sixteen stage crew, three flymen, six electricians and two sound engineers would be working from eleven at night to eight in the morning taking out the previous production. For the first week the production crew would be working two shifts, day and night.

Over the next week, while the cast re-rehearsed *Part One*, the production team would be following a baffling schedule: they would paint the droom, build the proscenium bridge, build the portcullis, pick up the tower on hoists, lower it into a hole, put in the cabling for the video and neon lighting on the droom floor and droom top... the list went on and on. A week later the cast would be turning up – in costume, make-up, wigs, masks – for the first day of the technical rehearsal.

The next Saturday, the grey sky and grey Thames perfectly matched the grey concrete of the National. Inside the building there were signs along the corridors and staircases pointing to 'Olivier Stage Left', 'Olivier Stage Right', 'Drum Entrance' and 'Bridge Entrance'. In the

Above left: Victoria King, puppet maker *(CM)*

Above right: In the paint frame *(CM)*

stalls – where the audience usually sits – there were tables, lamps, leads, rows of computers, music stands, telephones, sandwiches, bottles of water and a bowl of fruit. Inside the auditorium, the atmosphere was the opposite to the one in the rehearsal room. It is a matter of professional courtesy in a rehearsal room that everyone concentrates on one piece of work at a time. Inside the Olivier six things were happening at once: painting, sawing, hammering, checking sound levels, adjusting lights and laying new bits of floor. Most people had headphones on. The lighting technicians wore mini miners' lamps. The airwaves were full of information: "Whoever is in the revolve, we're going to rotate…"

Sprays of sparks descended from a high grid, where a pair of legs could be seen dangling. As soon as one person put down a sheet of flooring someone else came and painted it. The lighting designer, Paule, walked round the stage with a walkie-talkie calling out numbers to her assistant. Each of the hundreds of lights in the theatre has a number (and when Paule went to bed at night all she could hear in her head were numbers, numbers, numbers). The sound assistant was checking levels and counting out his own numbers: "one-two-three-four-five-six." The sound designer, Paul Groothuis, was playing gun-shots, a goose, Oxford traffic, a zeppelin, wolves growling, polar bears grunting and bells ringing. Most people carried torches, for when the lighting plot changed and the stage was suddenly pitched into darkness. As all this went on, the designer, Giles, quietly walked back and forth across a set that only a couple of months ago had been a model in his studio in Kilburn.

As an adult, Philip Pullman had fallen in love with the toy theatres sold at Pollocks, the theatre shop in Covent Garden. Imagine if Pollocks were able to sell a toy version of the Olivier, complete with the set for *His Dark Materials*. If Pullman had bought that theatre, taken the box home and emptied the contents on to the floor, dozens and dozens pieces would have fallen out. The accompanying

instruction leaflet would have to be a small book, about the length of *Lyra's Oxford*, and would need to include a glossary for the names.

The *sliders* were black flats that slid in from either side of the stage. The *portcullis* was the main backdrop that flew down from the tower. The *rim revolve* carried the bench, the Oxford colleges, the Trollesund trees and the snowbridge round the front of the stage. Scenes were played on the top of the *drum revolve* – Lord Asriel's fortress, the cafe at Cittàgazze. Others were played inside the drum revolve, in the *droom* – the Retiring Room, Mrs Coulter's London home, the rusty old hulk, the Bolvangar canteen and the laboratory with the daemon separator. The *proscenium bridge* was a walkway high above the stage and ran from one side to the other. It was from here that the Bolvangar searchlight tracks across the audience as Lyra is captured, and here that Lord Asriel and his snow leopard stand at the end of Part One and deliver the lines from *Paradise Lost:*

> "Into this wild Abyss, the wary fiend
>   Stood on the brink of Hell and looked a while,
>   Pondering his voyage…"

Above: Robert Butler with Paul Groothuis (sound designer) *(CM)*
Opposite: Costume designs by Jon Morrell *(CM)*

In the rehearsal room there had been fifty images Blu-tacked to the wall, showing the scenes that make up *Part One*. When Nick had seen these, he had said, "Well, we're giving them their money's worth." The question was whether it was possible to get the images to join together on stage as seamlessly as they had when he had flicked through the sheets of the story board. He had given himself four days to put these fifty scenes together. For these four days he would sit in the middle of the stalls, close to the set designer, the costume designer, the lighting designer, the production manager, and the composer. Nick picked up the microphone. "Is this working?" he asked. ("Yes," came back the answer.) "Hello, everybody." For the next four days the *everybody* he was talking to – on stage, back stage, in the stalls, and over the tannoys in their dressing rooms – would hear this monologue of Nick on the microphone.

Each moment in the Technical would be a trade-off between getting things right (for safety reasons, for artistic reasons) and running out of

time. Nick's tone was mostly courteous, but as one delay followed another, it wasn't hard to hear patience battling it out with frustration. From the first moment of the technical there were things that suddenly didn't work in the way they had in the rehearsal room.

Before the lights came up, Anna, Dominic and Sam stepped through a central door in the middle of the portcullis, walked downstage (closer to the audience) and sat on the green bench in the dappled light beneath a tree.

"Will…," said Anna.

"Lyra…," said Dominic.

Sam appeared with the pine marten and said, "Say something". Sam and the pine marten appeared at the same time, and Sam placed the pine marten in Lyra's lap.

"Okay," said Nick, over the microphone, "Let's hold it there."

Under the stage lighting, it was suddenly impossible to see Pantalaimon, as his colours blended with Lyra's summer dress. Aletta quickly arranged a new entrance for the daemon. Sam would stay behind the tree for as long as possible while Pantalaimon curled round its trunk and talked to Lyra. This way the pine marten stood out vividly against the tree trunk, allowing the audience to get used to the idea of Pantalaimon before they had to get used to the idea of a puppeteer in black costume and mask. Nick said, "If we can get the first few seconds right, and get the audience to accept the idea of daemons, I don't think there'll be a problem."

Over the next three days of the Technical they made slow progress. Nick established some principles for scene changes. "What we know is that everything is allowed a maximum amount of time and anything that can't be done in that time has to be modified." He frequently stopped and went back over a scene change to see if the transition could be quicker. "It sounds like I'm being really picky," he said, "but it's that kind of thing that gives it momentum. Those are the things that make all the difference."

Decisions were taken quickly, and some bits that didn't work were immediately cut. When the Gyptians appeared in the rusty old hulk, Nick said, "There's a hell of a lot of generalised banging of pots and pans. Let's cut the pots and pans. I'm not interested in cooking any more." When they reached the Bolvangar canteen he cut some stage business to do with the handing out of pills. "I'm sorry folks, I'm really really sorry, but we're going to cut the pills. The clock is ticking and we haven't got time to finesse this. Let's press on." When the Gyptians went on their journey up to Bolvangar, they had to walk through the trees (the polystyrene and steel ones) on the rim revolve. They had a sledge they were taking with them. It was going to be too time-consuming to work out a way of getting the sledge, which was also on the rim revolve, past the trees on the rim revolve, so it was cut. It would appear, later, in Lord Asriel's fortress as set-dressing. Other scenes had to be gone over again and again. When Tony Costa and Ben save Lyra from the Tartar Guards, the two actors made their entrance through the stalls. "This is the only time we do this," said

Above: Emily Mytton/Stelmaria *(IK)*

Nick, "and I'm sorry to say that I don't buy that." A new entrance had to be swiftly devised.

Sometimes the delays would take on an air of mystery. "Why are we waiting?" Nick asked. (The stage manager explained.) "How long will it take?" (The stage manager told him.) Ten minutes later, Nick asked, "What are we waiting for?" (The stage manager told him that something couldn't be done.) "Why can't it? There's always a solution. We can always do something."

All the time, Nick was driving the technical rehearsal forward. Here was an optimist coming up against every teething problem a new production could offer. The portcullis began to lean. The droom began to lean. Bits of scenery collided with one another. Nick sat in the middle of the stalls with a microphone: everyone could hear him and he wanted to hear from them. As the delays continued, one after another, it was never any one person's fault, it was always a new problem. Three years of work had narrowed down to a very limited number of hours: it felt like a struggle between man and machinery.

At times, directing a play seemed as lonely a job as writing in a shed. "Am I making any sense?" Nick asked. There was silence. "Can I assume someone's going to do that?" More silence. "Can someone please say something?"

It was a little like the quotation at the front of *Northern Lights*: there was Nick staring into the abyss; there were the dark materials, mixing confusedly; out of these he had to create new worlds. As he stood in the darkness of the stalls, he might have been standing on the brink of hell (or hell, for a theatre director), looking a while, and pondering his voyage.

● ● ●

THE FIRST PREVIEW, scheduled for Thursday 4 December, had to be cancelled as they had simply run out of time. The new plan was to run

Part One on Friday afternoon and preview that evening. Nick had invited a couple of hundred people from around the National to watch the dress rehearsal, which began at 1.30pm. They saw more than they had bargained for.

The most dramatic moment came when two huge pieces of scenery moved inexorably towards one other like a slow-motion car-crash. The drum revolve had been turning in one direction (it looked like one half of a cake sitting on the stage), and the portcullis, which should have flown up into the tower by now, was still down, touching the stage. As the drum revolve ground into the portcullis there was an awful creaking sound. "Stop!" "Stop!" "Stop!" went the shouts. The actors were immediately asked to leave the stage. *As quickly as possible.* The production manager, Sacha, hurried on, saying, "Nobody do anything till we see what the situation is..."

When one of the witches is tortured by Mrs Coulter, and Mrs Coulter breaks the witch's finger, another of the actors on stage makes the agonising sound of the fingers breaking by twisting some bubble wrap. It could have been the soundtrack for the whole afternoon. A twist of the bubble wrap for the moment when a dresser couldn't find her way to the drum revolve. Another twist of the bubble wrap when the slider refused to slide. And another twist when an actor, waiting for the make-up artist to arrive, missed his entrance. The most worrying aspect was that some very important timings involving large pieces of stage machinery had never worked first time. The dress rehearsal took four and a half hours. Nick warmly thanked the audience for their support and promised them, "It's going to be better than this." He bounded on to the stage to thank the actors and told them that evening's show, the second preview, had also been cancelled. The decision had only been taken a few minutes before.

It's an article of faith in the theatre that the show must go on, but there are times when the show mustn't go on. In large theatres that use dangerous machinery, the safety of the actors and the stage crew is paramount. The welfare of the audience is very important too: if they had to sit through another four and a half hour performance they would have left the theatre at midnight, exhausted and miserable.

During rehearsals, Nick had sometimes referred to the MGM school of acting. When young starlets arrived at the Hollywood studio in the 1930s and 40s, they were given a guidebook to acting. The most important advice concerned the way to answer the telephone. If the news they were about to hear was going to be bad, the starlet was encouraged to approach the phone with a happy face, pick up the phone in a breezy manner, and brightly say, "Hello!" (Then, as the bad news was delivered, her face could fall.) Conversely, if the news was going to be good, the starlet should approach the phone in a gloomy, listless manner so that when the good news came, her face could light up.

There was no better demonstration of the MGM school of acting than the faces of the audience as they entered the National Theatre foyer on Friday evening. Hundreds and hundreds of people, many of them parents and children, arrived at the theatre ready to be the very first to see *His Dark Materials – Part One*. A row of diplomatic and understanding employees of the National – the front of house manager, the press officers, the general manager, the marketing manager, the executive director, the contracts manager, the box office manager, the director's assistant – stood in the foyer, greeting members of the public. They said they were terribly sorry... there had been insuperable technical difficulties... here was a voucher for free drinks... tickets would be rearranged for another performance... The expressions of hundreds of members of the public went from MGM happy to MGM sad. "Let's go and see *Master and Commander*", one man said to wife and children, referring to the new Russell Crowe movie, "They can't cancel that."

Backstage, several actors said, "At least it's good for your book." Everyone knew bad news made good copy; the only trouble was, the

Opposite: Katy Odey/Lady Salmakia *(IK)*

news wasn't that bad. Or not nearly bad enough to make good copy. It was miserable for the audiences that two previews had been cancelled. The whole company were clearly upset about that. But in terms of the prospects for *His Dark Materials*, whether or not this enterprise would succeed, it was not necessarily a mortal blow.

In a month's time the cancellations would be a footnote in the show's history. At this stage my view was that a genuine crisis would be:

- if the audience could not follow the story;
- if the audience did not warm to Anna;
- if the audience thought the puppeteers in black costumes and masks looked ridiculous;
- if the audience liked the beginning, quite liked the middle and were bored by the end.

It is nearly always possible to solve technical problems. They are fixable. It would have been very hard, this late in rehearsals, to solve artistic ones.

On the next day, Saturday afternoon, the cast had a second dress rehearsal. There were still delays; but it was encouraging. At the very

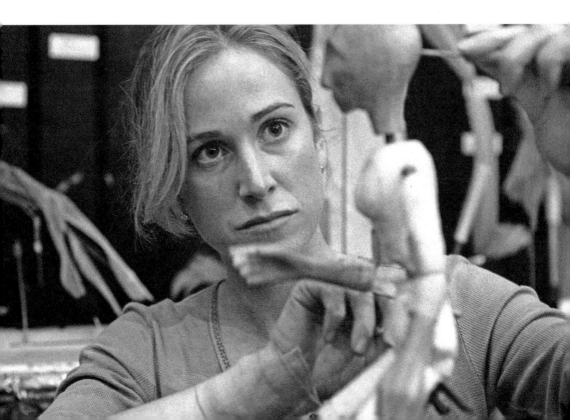

end, Nick spent five minutes working out a very quick curtain call – just for the evening.

Over supper in the canteen Nick said he was going to make a speech telling the audience that there might be stops. Nicholas Wright was sitting next to him and said he was looking forward to an audience. He wondered if any of the characters might get booed. Perhaps the President would be. Or, if not the President, his emissary from Geneva, Fra Pavel, the snaky one who picks his nose on his first entrance. It was impossible to know how an audience might react.

Over at the National Film Theatre next door, Paule, Aletta and Giles were having a drink and talking about anything but the show. It would be a nerve-wracking evening, especially for Giles, who later said that if the show had stopped in the way it had at the dress rehearsal, it would have been like having an egg broken on his head and feeling it run very very slowly down his face.

Backstage, the announcement came over the tannoy. "Ladies and gentlemen, the house is now open. Please do not cross the stage. The house is now open." In the auditorium, Philip Pullman and his wife, Jude, took their seats in the centre of the stalls. The story that he had first started writing ten years ago was about to be replayed back to him. Some members of the audience spotted him and asked for autographs. Others spotted the star of *Billy Elliot* sitting on the other side of the aisle.

At 7.30pm Nick walked to the front of the stage, introduced himself and explained that a couple of days ago he had read in an article that the idea of staging Philip Pullman's trilogy was "insanely ambitious". He had to say the article was right. This was the first performance of *His Dark Materials* and it should have been the third. He had to warn the audience that they had not yet managed to run the show without having to stop. That might well happen this evening. If it did, his assistant would announce that the show had stopped, and then,

probably about a minute later, that it was starting again. Nick said he hoped everyone would enjoy Philip Pullman's fantastic story.

The house lights went down. In the dark, Anna, Dominic and Sam walked through a door in the portcullis and took their positions on the bench in the Botanic Garden. The dappled lights came up, the music faded, the bells struck twelve times for midnight, and the first thousand members of an audience for *His Dark Materials* heard the first words from two people living in parallel universes, one of whom has a daemon.

"Will," said Anna.

"Lyra," said Dominic.

Sam moved the pine marten round the trunk of the tree.

"Say something," said Sam.

● ● ●

Above: Dominic Cooper *(IK)*

Chapter Six

"**adventure.** *noun.* 1a. an undertaking involving danger, risks, and uncertainty of outcome. b. an exciting or remarkable experience. 2. an enterprise involving financial risk."
The Penguin English Dictionary

A group of 30 A-level students – media studies, drama, English – filed into the circle seats in the Olivier, sat down, and stared at a rowing boat on an almost empty stage. The boat sat in a pile of white circles, like ripples, near some collapsible canvas chairs and low tables. An eery sound, like an Arctic wind, only more desolate, was blowing round the theatre.

Above: Anna Maxwell Martin *(IK)*

It was lunchtime, a week after the first preview, and the students were on a tour of the National Theatre. The tour guide, Anna Glover, was explaining to the group the difference between the National and the West End. The main one, said Anna, was that the National was subsidised, which meant it was not solely driven by box office considerations. Unlike commercial managements in the West End, the National Theatre had greater freedom to experiment and take artistic risks. As the students looked down at the rowing boat, they were staring at one of the greatest risks the National had taken. In the words of one veteran stage manager, it was the biggest show they had done in 20 years.

Of course, Anna explained, the theatre also had greater responsibilities. This was a national theatre and its professed aim was to be national with a small 'n'. *His Dark Materials* was an example of this: it was aimed at all age groups, especially teenagers, with reduced ticket prices for under-18s at all performances, and reduced rates for school and college groups.

It was only possible for the National to attempt to capture the worlds of *His Dark Materials* because the Olivier had enormous technical capability. As Anna explained how the drum revolve and the rim revolve worked, the drum came up, and it and the rim revolve rotated 180 degrees. Everything she was trying to explain was happening as effortlessly as if she had cued the revolves herself.

It had gone nearly as smoothly the previous Saturday. The first preview of *His Dark Materials* had run without a single stop. So had the second preview. But there was no time to pause, and the day after the second performance of *Part One* the company began the technical rehearsal for *Part Two*. Nick had already decided to give himself more time for this technical rehearsal and cancelled the first preview of *Part Two* that would have been on the Saturday night. Three previews had been lost in total. "With hindsight, I should have scheduled more

time," said Nick in a press statement. "I apologise unreservedly to the people we've had to turn away.

The technical rehearsal for *Part Two* began with an opening montage recapping the storyline from *Part One* (a sort of MTV type of storytelling), then plunged into a crisis meeting of the Church once it has discovered Lyra's secret name. Soon Will was cutting a window into Lord Boreal's study to retrieve the alethiometer and Lord Asriel was collecting an army to fight the Authority. The tiny Gallivespians had made their first entrance, speaking in the clipped accents of a 1940s war movie. The angels had floated on, using the genteel tones of Savile Row tailors. The witches had gathered in the mountains… Mrs Coulter had set up camp… Will had met his father… the President had been told about the possibility of a bomb… the Technical was

Above: Dominic Cooper *(IK)*

speeding along. It had taken two and a half days to reach the setting that was facing the A-level students when they had slipped into the Olivier – a rowing boat on a stage. It looked a modest affair, but this boat would be taking Lyra and Will to the Land of the Dead.

If the students could have walked behind the boat and seen what lay backstage (which is off-limits for tours during productions) they would have come across nearly every other scene in the two plays. It was as if the whole story had been packed into an attic until there was no more room. The life-size angels rested against some shelves, which contained the three Gallivespians, the rodent daemons, and the bears' heads. Several cloudpines and a snow leopard leant against a table, a row of bulrushes sat on the floor next to banks of lights, and towering green cliffghasts loomed next to the dark Trollesund trees. The faded cladding of the rusty old hulk stood side by side with the gleaming corrugated hut where the severed daemons are kept.

Every prop told a bit of the story. Two alethiometers lay next to a leather folder, which had a label next to it saying 'Lyra's Secret Name Document'. It was this folder that Brother Joseph hands to the President at the beginning of *Part Two*. Inside was a sheet of paper typed up by the props department with rules from the Consistorial Court of Disciple. No-one in the audience would ever see the rules, which included: "Listen to Your Superiors and obey unquestioningly". At the bottom of this formal document, someone had put an asterisk and written in pencil: "Her name is Eve!" Also on the table was a plastic bowl with rice, tomatoes and grated cheese. You would search in vain through the 1300 pages of *His Dark Materials* to find the scene in which these were props. It was someone's lunch.

The sound designer, Paul, sat at his computer at the back of the stalls, playing with the weather conditions for the Land of the Dead. He had two main sources for the desolate Arctic sound. One had been a gap in a door at the very top of the National. Paul had gone up there during a storm and recorded the wind whistling through the crack. The other source was Paul himself. He had made the sound of the wind by blowing through his lips, recording it, and putting some 'reverb' on it. He was sitting behind banks of highly sophisticated sound equipment and the sound effect he was using for one of the most moving sections of the story could have been made by a five-year-old. Sound designers often make their own effects. Another one Paul had made was used in the show, and he rubbed the palms of his hands together to demonstrate. He had recorded the sound of his hands rubbing together and speeded it up to become the wings of the dragonflies that transport the Gallivespians.

●　●　●

THEY WERE WORKING in the dark, about a dozen of them, dressed in black, moving swiftly and quietly, with the aid of a couple of pinpoint torchlights. The blue lighting gave their shirts a burgundy tinge. To judge by their stealth these guys might have been bank robbers or smugglers.

The Olivier stage crew were setting up Scene 32 while, only a few feet away, Scene 31 was unfolding in front of the first ever audience for *Part Two*. Only the portcullis divided the scene in the light from the scene in the dark. As quietly as they could, the crew had slid a rowing boat into the centre of the stage, lifted it over some fabric painted with white circles, and bolted the boat on to its base. The crew flattened out the ripples so when the base of the boat rose into the air, the ripples would fan out like the hoops of a crinoline. As they busied round the boat, the production manager, Sacha, glanced anxiously at the monitor, to check what point the actors had reached in the scene being played on the other side of the backdrop.

On the monitor, by the stage right door, Sacha could see Mrs Coulter on stage telling the President that she was protecting her daughter from "a body of men with a feverish obsession with sex". Minutes before, Patricia Hodge had rushed through the stage right door, dipping her head under some low scaffolding wrapped in foam, closely followed by her dresser, who simultaneously slipped Mrs Coulter's coat over Patricia's shoulders as a stage manager handed Patricia a handbag. Mrs Coulter was about to enter the Consistorial Court of Discipline. Only a few minutes before, she had been on stage, in Scene 27, wearing a safari suit and with her hands in chains.

As Mrs Coulter was telling the President that the Authority is useless and the greatest kindness would be "to seek him out and give him the gift of death", the rowing boat was securely fastened to the base. John Carlisle, playing the Boatman, crossed the backstage area in the darkness and stepped gingerly into the boat. At the end of Mrs Coulter's scene, the sound desk cued in the eery wind, and John took the oars in his hands and waited as the base of the tower moved fifteen feet up into the air. The oars had been illuminated like glowsticks on fireworks night. All anyone could see from backstage, was a pair of yellow oars rising higher and higher in the darkness.

On the monitor, Sacha could see Perkins, the official on the outskirts of the Land of the Dead, telling Lyra and Will that they would have to wait till they died before they could make the journey. Lyra and Will met the families, who sat on low collapsible chairs on the other side of the stage, waiting for their Deaths to call them. Backstage, they could hear the sound of waves hitting the shore. As the portcullis, which had separated the stage crew from the audience, went up, the Boatman was revealed, in the centre of the stage, and halfway up in the air. He wore a dark suit and bowler hat, and lights shone on his face and his oars, as he rowed gently towards Lyra and Will. He was accompanied on his journey by the haunting sound of a trombone. As the boat moved towards Will and Lyra, the revolve moved round and the tower lowered.

Lyra and Will told the Boatman that they wanted to go to the Land of the Dead and they wanted to come back, too. John's craggy face greeted the request with weary amusement. "How many people do you think I've taken across this lake? Millions. Millions, millions."

And then came one of the most heart-rending events in the story. All through rehearsals Nick had been looking for moments where the bond between Lyra and Pantalaimon could be made to look unbreakable. Early on in *Part One*, when Roger had been abducted by the Gobblers, Lyra tells Pantalaimon that without Roger, "It's like I'm only half of meself." Pantalaimon replies, "You still got me." Lyra says, "Yeah." She takes the daemon in her hands and lifts him towards her face. "I'd die if I didn't," she adds. The bond couldn't be closer. By the time the Boatman has arrived, Lyra's determination to find Roger forces her to say goodbye to Pantalaimon. On stage an actor was saying goodbye to a puppet and in the auditorium there were members of the audience in tears.

Above: Anna Maxwell Martin *(IK)*

About 500 years ago, a woman had her portrait painted, holding an animal that looked like an elegant weasel. The artist had made the animal bigger than it actually was, for the sake of the composition. The woman is calm and serene and looks away into the distance. The animal, which is an ermine, rests on her arms, and looks in roughly the same direction. There is a sense of trust between the two of them, as if they are sharing the same mood, looking at the same thing, sharing the same thoughts, as if – in a way – they are at one. It has been described as the first picture in Western art to penetrate the inner feelings of the sitter; it's as if the animal brings us closer to understanding the person. The picture of the *Lady with an Ermine* by Leonardo da Vinci had been an inspiration to Pullman in creating the idea of daemons. So a picture that now hangs in Cracow in Poland had contributed to the anguish unfolding on stage, as Pantalaimon screamed after Lyra, as the boat pulled away.

Outside, on one of the stage left staircases, the three Harpies were having final adjustments made to their black chiffon costumes and the vast wings that fold round them like a tent. When Cecilia Noble, who plays No-Name, the main harpy, had first read the part during the summer workshop, she had delivered the lines with a ferocity and attack that took everyone by surprise; she read as if each word was written in capitals and had an exclamation mark. Nick's response to this reading, was uncompromising. "Fantastic," he said, "That's the style of acting this show requires. Those sharp edges."

Six months later, Cecilia was having to watch the tips of her wings: as she moved from the landing to the stage left entrance, they were catching the top of the door. As she walked down the corridor – past the smelly leather costumes of the bears hanging on a rack – she had to take care the tips of her wings didn't knock the fire sprinklers on the ceiling.

When Lyra and Will reach the Land of the Dead, a mirror is lowered to fill the stage. The first idea had been to reflect the audience in the mirror so that it looked as they were peopling the Land of the Dead, but it hadn't been possible to get the angle right. A number of the actors, in grey caps, ties, shorts, socks, shoes, coats appeared from all round the auditorium as children, and started climbing past members of the audience. The house lights had come up a little, to include the audience in the scene.

The last child to appear was Roger, walking down the centre aisle. "Lyra! I knew you'd come…" For Russell Tovey, as Roger, to reach the stage he had to climb over three rows of seats. One worry that the two Nicks, the director and the adapter, had had when they were discussing the story over the last year was whether, across the six hours, the audience would remember who Roger was. Who was this character who compels Lyra to visit the Land of the Dead? In rehearsals, Nick had said that worry had evaporated thanks to the forceful way Russell had stamped his character on our imagination.

In the last few minutes there had been several of these moments: John's mordant humour as the Boatman; Cecilia's rasping glee as she flapped her wings and tormented Will about his mother; and Russell climbing over the seats to greet Lyra ("I've been calling for you ever since I died.") This was high definition acting – vivid characters against a dramatic landscape. It was the style Nick had wanted to aim for on the first day of rehearsals, when he mentioned the two Charles Dickens novels that David Lean had filmed.

Two and a half hours earlier, the cast had stood in the wings, waiting for the montage that opens *Part Two*. In the blue half-light, with the monitors showing the empty stage, the President held his snake round his arm, the witches clung to their cloudpines, and Tullio bent over and touched his toes. As the music started, Lyra rushed on, and said "Run, Pan! Run!", then Lord Asriel looked into the Aurora and said, "Look at that pathway…" and Mrs Coulter pulled away from him. Timothy Dalton exited stage right in flowing trenchcoat, dipping his head under the piping with the foam wrapping. He was closely followed by Emily

Mytton, the puppeteer for Stelmaria, who handed her snow leopard daemon to a stage manager, who hung it against the shelves. Patricia Hodge exited stage right (in her fur coat) after staying to ask the President for permission to keep her daughter… Will told Lyra he was looking for his dad… Jopari told Lee Scoresby that only the bearer of the knife could kill the Authority… and in no time, Emily was back, this time dressed in purple ecclesiastical robes to play the stenographer in the Grand Chamber of the Consistorial Court of Disciple. So many story lines!

And behind all these stories, there was another story, far bigger than that of a young girl looking for love, which underpinned both the plays and the novels. This story was more in the way of a few anecdotes and observations that had appeared in a short essay in 1810. A century later this essay had been described as the most perceptive piece of philosophy since Plato. In the 1970s the essay was translated from German into English and published in the *Times Literary*

Above: Patricia Hodge and Timothy Dalton *(IK)*

Supplement. One of the people who read that week's edition of the *TLS* was an English teacher living in Oxford. "I can't tell you," he has said, "what an impression that essay made on me."

Twenty years later, the teacher and part-time writer had become an ex-teacher and a full-time writer. He wrote a trilogy of novels on a similar theme to the essay, yet admitted that the essay said "in three or four pages what I had to say in 1300 or so, and says it better." Heinrich von Kleist's essay 'On the Marionette Theatre' was written in a conversational style, and began with an evening encounter between a writer and a friend who had recently seen a puppet show. The friend loved the puppets for their complete absence of self-consciousness. This prompted the writer to tell an anecdote about how a beautiful young man that he knew had become aware of his looks and how this knowledge had destroyed the beauty. The writer's friend told him another anecdote about fencing with a bear in Russia finding that whenever he feinted with his rapier, the bear didn't flinch. It is impossible to deceive a bear. The essay linked this to what happened when Adam and Eve were expelled from the Garden of Eden. As they moved towards self-consciousness they lost their state of grace. This was the story, the story of the Fall, that the company of *His Dark Materials* were about to complete for the very first time.

There were things the company had learnt from performing *Part One* that had been essential for them to remember in *Part Two*. After the first two previews Nick had given notes. There were various points he had needed to make that applied to specific scenes: characters wearing wide-brimmed hats should make sure their faces were visible. They should tilt their hats up or take them off when playing to the 'raked' auditorium (one that slopes upwards). When mentioning other characters' names, especially when it is a new character, the actors should make the name absolutely clear, to help those members of the audience who didn't know the story or hadn't bought a programme. The blade in the daemon separator needed to be more visible. It would be lowered a little and Dr Sargent would point it out with a line or two that Nicholas Wright said he would add. "I'll do some radio writing."

The Gyptians' accents had been so authentic in the first preview that few people could understand what they were saying. At the second preview the accents had been lighter. Various steps were being taken to minimise the amount of noise backstage during the scenes. Some cumbersome pieces of set dressing would be replaced by other bits which weren't. For instance, the double windows in Mrs Coulter's London home, which had to be bolted onto the walls of the droom, would be replaced by a pair of curtains that could simply be hung.

Mrs Coulter's first entrance continued to trouble Patricia Hodge. There were a number of difficulties. "The fur coat is number one," she said to Nick, during the note session, "Getting it through the doorway is a triumph." When the door was open, it blocked off some of the audience on her right hand side. There was also the problem – recognised way back in the summer – that when Mrs Coulter makes her first entrance, so does the Golden Monkey. It affects where the audience focuses and who the actor watches. "It's split-focus," she said, "The second I look at Lyra she has to look at the monkey. You can't make an entrance with a fur coat and a monkey. It's *hell*." She said, "You have to feel sorry for me." "Not really," said Nick, "It's all fixable."

There were also more general points about the first two previews that would apply just as much (if not more) to *Part Two*. Nick wanted the cast to include the audience as much as they felt they realistically could, by finding moments when they could turn their heads, and so share the story. The phrase was: *embracing the house.* The actors needed to draw the audience in and not always talk too directly and intently to one another. It is a delicate balance to achieve this and also to appear natural. "Let me be very blunt about playing a story that is this big," Nick said, "in a theatre that is this big. If you feel happy bringing the audience in, they will feel happy too. They will embrace you more if you find ways of embracing them."

Nick said to Anna that, whatever dangers Lyra is facing, she has to stay positive, to relish each challenge. Nick warned the actors to be "very careful not to go melancholy because the audience is quick to go in that direction." After two previews he could see what the audience's expectations were about *His Dark Materials*. "It's very very plain that the audience hasn't come to laugh," he said, "They've come for a sad story. If you play anything that's sad or doleful, that's where they'll go."

● ● ●

ACTORS DON'T GET to see the show they're in. Twelve weeks of rehearsals and they will never know what it is like to watch *His Dark Materials*. In the wings, they crowded the monitors, watching in silence as (for the first time) the six hour play reached its climax. Iorek was standing in his armour and mask, next to Serafina Pekkala with her witch's rags and amber spyglass, who was standing next to Dr Sargent in his white coat, who was standing next to Perkins, the sneering official from the Land of the Dead. On the small screen they watched Will and Lyra come across a casket with a decrepit old man inside. It was the Authority and he was dying. Earlier that day there had been Christmas Carols in the foyer of the theatre. Now the theatre was presenting a scene depicting the death of God.

The newspapers had carried articles in which the production was attacked for its timing and poor taste. Pullman told the *Independent*, "This is the National Theatre, not the National Christian Theatre." He said his books celebrated love, courage, intellectual curiosity and kindness, and condemned cruelty, intolerance and fanatical zealotry. Many people clearly agreed with him. Over the weekend Pullman's

trilogy had been voted Number 3 in the BBC's *Big Read*, and was only beaten by Tolkien and Jane Austen. It was a remarkable result since *His Dark Materials* has only existed as a trilogy for three years and has not reached its wide audience by becoming a major movie or TV series.

As Serafina Pekkala, Niamh Cusack brought a basket of blackberries for Will and Lyra. Niamh had been at the very first workshop a year before when there had only been bits and pieces of scenes to read and it had been impossible to know what sort of plays these would be. Serafina Pekkala had taken over the pivotal role Mary Malone plays in the books: introducing the idea of sexual love to Lyra by telling of her own love affair with Farder Coram. At the front of the stage, Lyra was kissing Will, and a stream of gold poured down over

Above: Niamh Cusack and Cecilia Noble *(IK)*

Serafina as she said, "two children are making love in an unknown world". Serafina was playing the role of the serpent in the Garden of Eden. In doing so, she was putting the plays (like the novels) firmly in the alternative tradition that believes Eve did the right thing. Many Christians would consider this heretical, but it is a heresy that runs through English literature and drama from Marlowe to Milton to Blake. (It has been said that the history of Europe is the history of heretics). Only by following the serpent's words did mankind begin its adventure.

After the night together, Lyra and Will were told by Serafina they had to close up the windows to prevent dust flowing away. They realised they could not live together. At the back of the stalls, the deputy stage manager watched as Will shattered the knife, and said, "LX cue 342. Go – Music cue 55. Go –", and the scene changed back to the Botanic Garden in the present day.

They had reached the last ten lines of the play, which explicitly state Pullman's theme. Will said, "There's no elsewhere…" Lyra said, "You must be where you are." Will said, "…and where you are is the place that matters most of all…" Lyra said, "'Cause it's the only place where you can make…" Will said, "…where you can build…" Lyra said, "…where you can share…" Together they said, "…the republic of heaven."

They got up from the bench, walked to opposite sides of the stage, turned and crossed back towards each other. As they did so, the music swelled and it looked as if they were going to meet half way. Perhaps at the last minute the sad ending would turn out to be a happy one. When they had rehearsed that moment, six months before in the summer workshop, Nick had said, "Dicking around with the audience is what we're about," and Pullman had laughed. But there was going to be no happy ending for the audience. Lyra and Will passed each other without any idea that they were so close. They were only inches apart on stage; in the story they were in parallel

universes. The deputy stage manager said, "LX cue 343 Go –" and the lights faded, and she said, "Flies cue 61. Go –" and the portcullis flew out, as the sliders pulled back and the tree divided in two and revolved round the stage. "LX Cue 344. Go." she said.

The lights came up on stage and the audience applauded. From the wings, the assistant stage manager watched the company take their bow. She could only see the back row of the actors in the bright light and hear the applause. The whole company took a bow. Timothy Dalton and Patricia Hodge took a bow. Anna and Dominic took a bow. Cheers and applause. The whole company took another bow. "We did it," said one actor, as she left the stage. The deputy stage manager said, "LX cue 345. Go." and the house lights came on.

A minute or two later, Nick was sitting in the stalls with Aletta, Giles, Jonathan, Paule, Paul, two assistant directors and several stage

Above: Dominic Cooper and Anna Maxwell Martin *(IK)*

managers. From their seats, they could see right through to the backstage wall with the bulrushes, Jordan College and the tree in the Botanic Garden. Nick had a pad with some notes. They had seventeen more performances, eight of *Part One,* nine of *Part Two,* before *His Dark Materials* opened to the press. Anna, Dominic and Sam had gone to the bar, along with Timothy Dalton, Patricia Hodge and others from the cast. Up at the bar, they were quietly celebrating the fact they had got through it at all. Here were three friends – Anna, Dominic and Sam – who had known each other for five years, and who between them were responsible for the emotional heart of the story. Meanwhile the director, designers, production team and stage managers went through the list of what needed to be done. A great deal was going to change between that night's preview and the press night. Nick raised the first thing he wanted to change. Someone explained what the problem had been.

Nick said, "Here's a suggestion…"

Above: Anna Maxwell Martin and Armoured Bears *(IK)*

The Cast, in alphabetical order

SAMUEL BARNETT . . . . Pantalaimon/Lyra's Death
JOHN CARLISLE . . . . Lord Boreal/Boatman
DOMINIC COOPER . . . . Will Parry
NIAMH CUSACK . . . . Serafina Pekkala
TIMOTHY DALTON . . . . Lord Asriel
PATRICK GODFREY . . . . Master of Jordan College/Farder Coram/
Giacomo Paradisi/Mother Jones' Death
STEPHEN GREIF . . . . John Faa/Bear/President of Consistorial Court
JAMIE HARDING . . . . Billy Costa/Paolo/Jones family
PATRICIA HODGE . . . . Mrs Coulter
AKBAR KURTHA . . . . Bearkeeper/Dr Cade
CHRIS LARKIN . . . . Stallholder/Iofur Raknison/Jopari
HELENA LYMBERY . . . . Salcilia/Hester/Jones Family/Harpy/Kirjava
TIM McMULLAN . . . . Fra Pavel/Lee Scoresby/Lord Roke
ANNA MAXWELL MARTIN . . . . Lyra Belacqua
IAIN MITCHELL . . . . Professor Hopcraft/Top-hatted man/
Dr Sargent/Bear
HELEN MURTON . . . . Macaw Lady/Daisy/Pipistrelle/Hannah Jones
EMILY MYTTON . . . . Stelmaria/Grimhild
CECILIA NOBLE . . . . Sister Betty/Ruta Skadi/No-Name
KATY ODEY . . . . Mrs Lonsdale/Sister Clara/Caitlin/
Lady Salmakia
NICK SAMPSON . . . . Thorold/Retired General/Balthamos
DANNY SAPANI . . . . Iorek Byrnison
JASON THORPE . . . . Ben/Cleric/Baruch
RUSSELL TOVEY . . . . Roger Parslow/Officer
DANIEL TUITE . . . . Cawson/Mayor/Cleric/Chevalier Tialys/
Perkins
ANDREW WESTFIELD . . . . Prof. of Astronomy/Dr West/Bear/
Lord Boreal's Butler/Jeptha Jones
BEN WHISHAW . . . . Kaisa/Brother Jasper
KATIE WIMPENNY . . . . Jessie/Grendella/Angelica
BEN WRIGHT . . . . The Golden Monkey/Tullio/Assistant Librarian
INIKA LEIGH WRIGHT . . . . Lily/Tortured Witch/Librarian/Harpy
RICHARD YOUMAN . . . . Tony Costa

The Production Team

Author of the books . . . . **PHILIP PULLMAN**
Author of the stage adaptation . . . . **NICHOLAS WRIGHT**

Director . . . . **NICHOLAS HYTNER**
Set Designer . . . . **GILES CADLE**
Costume Designer. . . . . **JON MORRELL**
Puppet Designer . . . . **MICHAEL CURRY**
Lighting Designer. . . . . **PAULE CONSTABLE**
Choreographer/Associate Director . . . . **ALETTA COLLINS**
Music . . . . **JONATHAN DOVE**
Assistant to the Composer . . . . **MATTHEW SCOTT**
Music Director . . . . **STEVEN EDIS**
Fight Director . . . . **TERRY KING**
Sound Designer . . . . **PAUL GROOTHUIS**
Video Projection Designer . . . . **THOMAS GRAY** for The Gray Circle
Computer Graphics Designer . . . . **YURI TANAKA** for The Gray Circle
Dialect Coach . . . . **JOAN WASHINGTON**
Company Voice Work . . . . **PATSY RODENBURG**
Staff Director. . . . . **MATT WILDE**

Assistant Staff Director **Dominic Leclerc**
Production Manager **Sacha Milroy**
Stage Manager **Courtney Bryant**
Deputy Stage Manager **Lesley Walmsley, Kerry McDevitt**
Assistant Stage Managers **Mary O'Hanlon, Brewyeen Rowland, Thomas Vowles, Dewi Wynne**
Costume Supervisor **Emma Marshall**
Puppet Supervisor **David Cauchi**
Video Realisation **Dick Straker** and **Sven Ortel** for Mesmer
Video Programming **Ian Galloway** for Mesmer
Video Operators and Realisation Assistants **Ian Galloway** and **Rupert Dean**
Keyboard Programming **Duncan Chave**
Assistant to the Lighting Designer **Cathy Joyce**
Assistant Production Managers **Gavin Gibson, Tom Richardson**
Music Programming **Duncan Chave**
Design Associates **Tim Blazdell, Will Bowen, Nick Murray**
Design Assistants **Geraldine Bunzl, Rachel Canning, Max Jones, Howard Lloyd**
Assistant Costume Supervisors **Hannah Trickett, Poppy Hall**
Production Photographer **Ivan Kyncl**
Publisher of the stage adaptation **Nick Hern Books** (www.nickhernbooks.co.uk)

His Dark Materials had its stage premiere at the National Theatre's Olivier Theatre
on 3 January 2004